EMBROIDERY TECHNIQUES FROM

EAST and WEST

EMBROIDERY TECHNIQUES FROM
EAST and WEST

TEXTURE AND COLOUR FOR QUILTERS AND EMBROIDERERS

Munni Srivastava

BATSFORD

**Dedicated to the master-weavers of Alaipura, Varanasi,
and to embroiderers, traditional and modern.**

This book is the culmination of two-and-a-half years of concentrated effort, building up a body of work for an exhibition, shared with the talented mosaicist, Elaine M. Goodwin, which took place in London in May 2001. The author would like to offer her most sincere thanks to several friends without whose support and encouragement the rewarding yet draining process of creating some forty textile pieces, while working full time, might never have taken place: Anne Dewe, Eduardo Hernandéz Martín, John Maxwell, Indu Patel, Terry Price and Alice Rugheimer. Between them, they offered support and kindnesses when the going got rough, patronage and encouragement. Special thanks are also due to Lindy Ayubi for much-appreciated nurturing during the London exhibition, to Elaine M. Goodwin for inspiration and much delightful laughter, to Joss Graham of Joss Graham Oriental Textiles for lending me transparencies, to Anna Steiner for invaluable advice and quiet support, to Caroline Taggart for her cheerful presence and to Satyendra Srivastava for bringing back from India a great mound of silk pieces, many of which went into the making of the works reproduced in this book. Patricia Brien of DMC, Paris, also deserves my gratitude for sending me great bags of luscious threads. Finally, thank you to Roger Huggins and Tina Persaud of B.T. Batsford for making this book happen.

Munni Srivastava, May 2001

All photography by Michael Wicks, except where otherwise indicated in the text.
Pieces shown on pages 6–7, 10, 29, 37 and 39 are reproduced by kind permission of Joss Graham.

First published 2001
This paperback edition published 2005

Text and original designs © Munni Srivastava 2001, 2005

The right of Munni Srivastava to be identified as Author of this work has been asserted by her in accordance with the Copyright, Designs and Patents Act 1988.

ISBN 0 7134 8954 5

A CIP catalogue record for this book is available from the British Library.

Printed in Singapore by Kyodo Printing Co. Ltd
for the publishers

B T Batsford
Chrysalis Books Group
The Chrysalis Building
Bramley Road
London W10 6SP
www.chrysalisbooks.co.uk

An imprint of **Chrysalis** Books Group plc

Contents

Introduction   8

Equipment   16
   Threads   18
   The Sewing Machine   20
   Fabrics   24

Hand Embroidery   26
   Mirror work – *Shisha*   28
   Other Hand Embroidery Stitches   32
   Kantha and other Quilting Traditions   36
     around the World
   Embroidery Motifs   43
   Other Embellishments   45

Machine Embroidery   46
Patchwork & Quilting   47
   Free-motion Machine Embroidery   48
   Appliqué   52
   Crazy Patchwork   55
   Cathedral Window Patchwork   56
   Strip Patchwork   58
   Tumbling Blocks   60
   Quilting   62
   Inspiration and Design   63

The Projects   66
   Cushion-making   116
   Wallhangings and Framed Pictures –
     Presentation and Conservation   122

Places to visit   127
Suppliers   127
Index   128

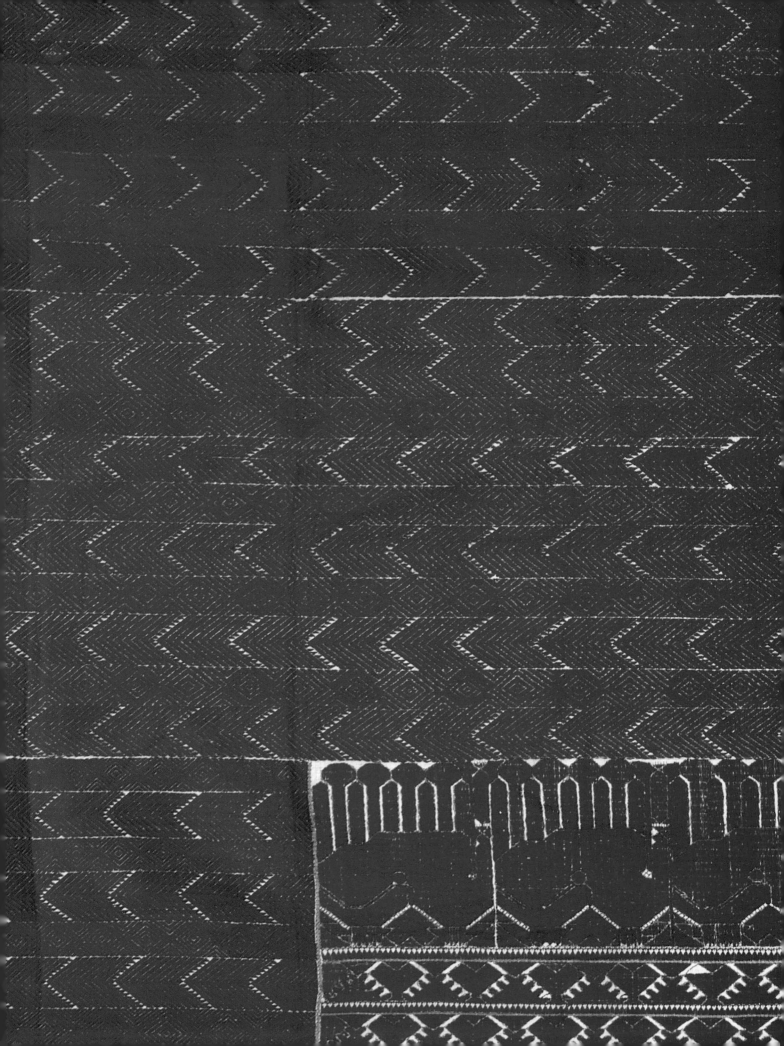

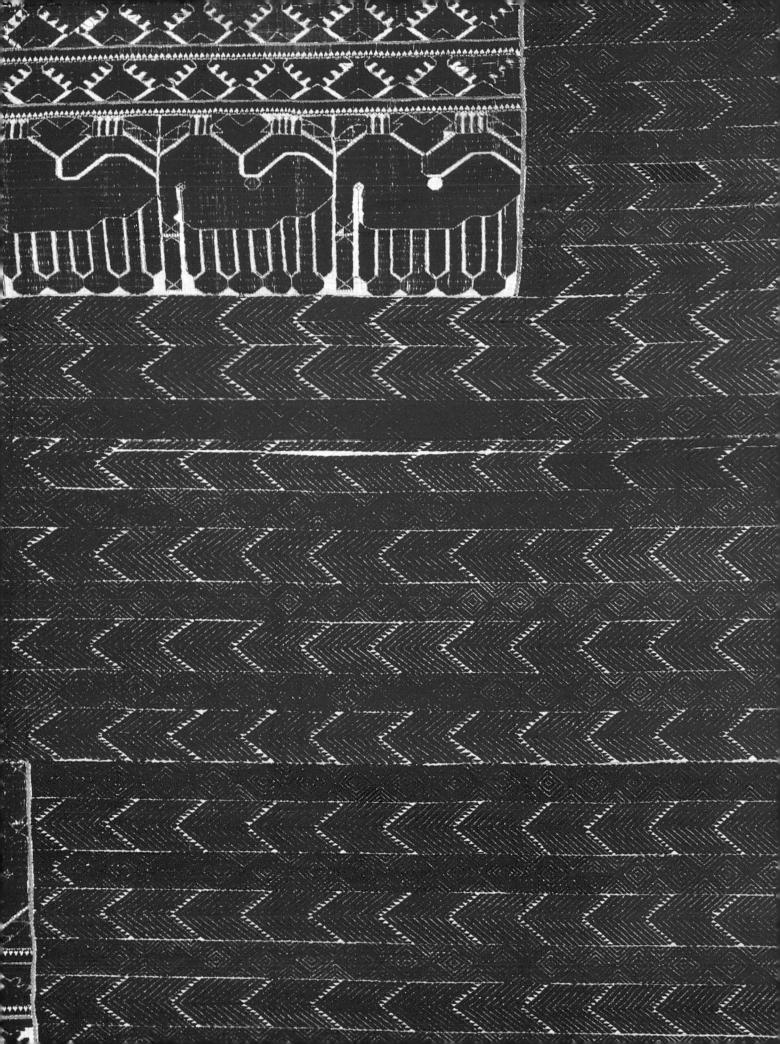

Introduction

This book is aimed at both embroiderers and quilters, and I hope that they will all be inspired to experiment with the style of embroidery I practise, which is a mixture of Indian and European techniques, including hand and machine embroidery, highlighted with beads and found objects. Hindu iconography, nature and poetry are recurring themes.

I use quilting as a way of creating a textured background to embroidery and appliqué (see, for example, the pieces reproduced on pages 85 and 93), and also in conjunction with crazy patchwork, which provides me with a beautiful canvas on which to project the embroidery (see pages 66 to 83). Quilting has long been a passion of mine, partly because of its universality – there are traditions of quilting in practically all parts of the world, including India – but also for the magical effect it has on surfaces. I work almost entirely with rich silks. Quilting catches the light and gives additional depth to colours. *Kantha* quilting, which originated in the Gujarat, Bihar and Bengal regions of India, and is still widely practised in these three Indian states, as well as in Bangladesh, is halfway between running-stitch embroidery and what a Westerner would understand as quilting. It can take the form of colourful folk art wallhangings or of bed coverings, worked over two or three layers of cotton fabric and adorned with naïve pictures portraying the everyday activities of village life or retelling popular religious tales. It is now also used to produce sophisticated and expensive pieces, such as the silk saris pictured on page 13, intended for an urban, well-to-do clientele. These were made in Bangladesh and are the result of the increasing cooperation between modern designers and skilled embroiderers – here, a women's cooperative in Dacca. The colours have been chosen to appeal to an urban, discriminating audience, but the motifs have kept their 'folksy' charm.

I use simple *kantha* quilting on its own (see, for example, *Entrapped Leaves II,* on page 113), or mixed with *shisha* (mirror) work, or with other embroidery, in the pieces worked over crazy patchwork. In *traditional* Indian embroidery, the combination of *shisha* and *kantha* quilting would only occur in Gujarat. Mirror work is a speciality of Gujarat, especially in Kutch, and of Rajasthan. It is widely used to brighten up clothing and decorate home furnishings. It is said to be auspicious, the mirrors deflecting the evil eye. Mirror work is not restricted to textiles; it is also used as a decorative feature in architecture, embedded in plaster and forming elaborate patterns, in village dwellings as well as in palatial buildings. In Gujarat, it is customary to hang strips of bunting with richly embroidered pennants over doorways as a sign of welcome. These pieces are known as *toran* (see page 10), and combine colourful embroidery with a floral or a religious theme and intricate mirror work. *Torans* are a stylized interpretation of the

Previous page. Red phulkari *from Punjab. This counted-thread technique uses a darning stitch to form geometric patterns that cover the background cloth almost entirely.*

Opposite page. Detail from the pallaw *– the ornate part of the sari with which the wearer traditionally covered her head. These expensive pieces originate from various parts of India and they reflect the influence of modern Indian textile designers on traditional artisans.*

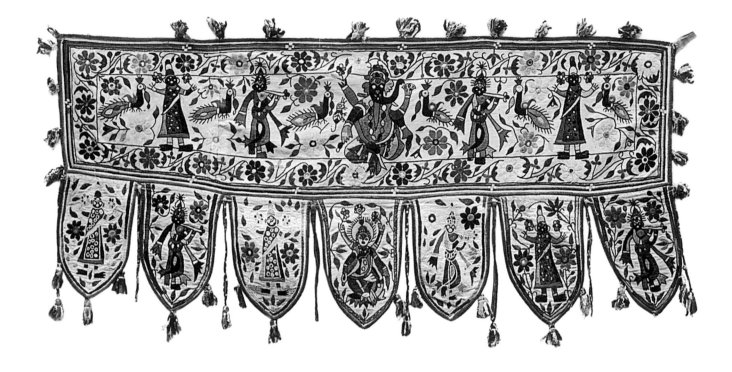

Above. Richly embroidered toran from Gujarat, showing religious figures and flowers. The small tassels, made of tiny strips of left-over fabric, are typical of Gujarat.

Opposite page. Details from a pale green summer sari and from a delicate table mat, all covered in chikan embroidery.

strings of mango leaves or of fragrant marigolds that are hung over doorways on festival days as a sign of welcome and a fertility symbol.

I undoubtedly owe my love of embroidery and of fabrics to my Indian background. As long as I can remember, I have been fascinated by the variety, the inventiveness, and the richness of both texture and colour of Indian textiles of all kinds. As a small child, I would watch my mother getting ready for an evening out or a grand wedding, draping a sumptuous Banaras gold brocade sari which formed sculptural folds around her slender shape. An entire district of the old city of Varanasi, where we lived, was occupied by handloom weavers. Narrow, poorly lit rooms were filled with the incessant clackety-clack sound of the looms. I'd stand for hours watching a weaver at work, the intricate glowing patterns forming slowly under his hands. It seemed pure magic! On trips to Lucknow, we'd always pay a visit to the Muslim artisans who produced the beautiful *chikan* embroidery – a type of shadow work done on diaphanous muslin – which is typical of the city. I was so anxious to grow up and get to wear these beautiful things and use them in my home.

The embroidery I now produce reflects the multifarious influences I have absorbed over the years. I have been fortunate to travel a lot during my life, and wherever I go, textiles

– traditional and modern – continue to fascinate me. American quilts, especially the soberly coloured, but intricately quilted Amish pieces, which put one in mind of a Mondrian painting, as well as the work of modern American art quilters, such as Libby Lehman, have been a great source of inspiration. The Mayan women in the uplands of Chiapas in Mexico, producing amazing textiles on hip looms while feeding babies or selling vegetables, gave me a sisterly feeling in the joy they took in their creations. One of them said: *'Pongo mis sueños en los tejidos'* (I put my dreams in my weaving). This statement from the mouth of a simple village woman was moving as well as humbling.

In India, while traditional artisans continue to make beautiful embroideries and textiles of all kinds, there is also a new breed of textile workers who collaborate with modern designers to produce beautiful work, combining traditional skills and materials with modern design and urban taste. This is an exciting development which, looking back at the 1960s to 1970s, seems almost miraculous. In those days, the emerging middle classes in India were often so enamoured of Western design as to dismiss the work of traditional artisans as old-fashioned. Easy-to-maintain synthetic fabrics were all the rage, and the lure of a Japanese polyester or a French silk chiffon sari was impossible to resist. This was an unfortunate trend for traditional embroiderers and other textile makers. The demand from abroad was often driven by a determination to obtain goods at prices so low that the artisan, pressed by local middlemen to meet these prices at any cost, either gave up the struggle or cut corners. The long-term prospects for these master craftsmen seemed grim. In recent years, however, a great change has taken place. With increased self-confidence, higher standards of living and better education, being Indian and championing Indian goods has become fashionable among the urban middle classes. Paradoxically, this change has coincided with the opening of India's economy to the world, for now that European goods have become much more available, they are no longer 'forbidden fruit', and the appreciation of home-produced goods has risen considerably. The collaboration with modern designers from India and abroad has resulted in a great flowering of talent among artisans of all kinds.

This book is the culmination of a period of two-and-a-half years spent building up a body of work destined for an exhibition in London. The technical sections at the beginning of the book do not claim to be exhaustive. I have only included the techniques I use in my own work. If you pick up this book as a keen quilter, you probably will not need to be told how to make tumbling blocks and cathedral window patchwork, but an embroiderer might. Similarly, the embroiderers among us will probably be familiar with many of the stitches I have included in the sampler. This is

Opposite page. Details from the pallaw *of two white silk saris, showing lavish* kantha *embroidery. The work is extremely fine; the choice of colours and the fine finish denote pieces destined for a sophisticated urban market.*

not important. The interesting part is to see what can be done with these techniques, and how they can be meshed together to produce exciting and challenging results.

I was a relative latecomer to machine embroidery. I now love it, especially when mixed with hand work and beading. Indian decorative artists of all kinds show an obsessive interest in surface texture and decoration. I am no exception! Use as much or as little ornamentation as suits your taste. Experiment with colour, and never stint on the quality of the materials used. While I am fascinated by the experimental work produced by textile artists whose soldering iron cohabits with their needlecase, I cannot go down that road. I use precious materials and spend an inordinate amount of time producing works which, I hope, will age gracefully and provide their owners with many years of pleasure.

If the most common question I'm asked at shows or exhibitions is, 'What shall I do if it gets dirty?', the next one must be, 'How long did it take you?' I find it difficult to explain that producing things quickly holds little appeal for me. I feel that the slow creative process, which acquires a momentum of its own and often evolves in a very different way from the piece envisaged at design stage, has a therapeutic effect on me. It is the perfect antidote to the stressful deadlines and the worries caused by a career in publishing! I often work at night as I listen to music or poetry, in the sole company of my much-loved cat. For me, this is the epitome of the joy of embroidering and hand-quilting. At the risk of sounding pompous, I must admit that I treasure the contemplative mood and the sense of continuity derived from the knowledge that generations of women, and men too, have contributed to this great tradition of stitched textiles and that I, too, can make my mark.

How to use this book

As you have probably realized, the type of work I produce crosses many boundaries and uses many techniques. Although I'm primarily an embroiderer, I also make patchwork and quilt, but always as a basis for my embroidery. I do hope embroiderers who have not done so previously will be tempted to experiment with patchwork and quilting techniques. These are discussed at the beginning of the book as general principles and explained in more detail in the instructions relating to the projects in which they are used. There are some wonderful books on the market that cover every aspect of patchwork and quilting, and it is not my purpose to compete with them.

Embellished patchwork is now a recognized discipline among the quilting fraternity and many art quilters mix disciplines to wonderful effect. I hope that embroiderers,

too, will feel inspired to introduce patchwork and quilting into their work. Indian and other techniques of hand embroidery are discussed in the first half of this book (see pages 26 to 42), as is free-machine embroidery (pages 46 to 51). On pages 43 and 44, you will find a variety of patterns drawn from traditional Indian motifs, which I have used in conjunction with crazy patchwork, free-motion machine embroidery, and random hand embroidery and beading.

Above. Detail from Night Blooms. *See complete piece on pages 94–5.*

The projects and their instructions begin on page 66. They are grouped according to the main techniques used. In order to avoid tedious repetitions, some of the instructions are cross-referenced from one project to another. I would strongly advise that if you want to embark on one of the crazy patchwork pieces, for example, you read not only the instructions relating specifically to it, but also those of *Indian Spring Memories,* on page 68, which is the first hanging of that series and contains the most detailed instructions. You may decide to replace one element used in a particular hanging with a different one. Indeed – and this is what I really hope you will do – you may opt to abandon the instructions altogether, design your own piece, choose those techniques which appeal to you particularly, mix them with your own and come up with a brand-new design idea! Similarly read up *Summer Sprites,* on page 84, before attempting *Dawn Blooms,* on page 90, or *Fragments,* on page 100, before tackling *Lost Continent* or *Adrift.*

There is a list of specialist suppliers at the end of the book. Many of these sell by mail order, so that you should be able to obtain the more outlandish supplies wherever you may live.

EQUIPMENT

Threads

A good tip to prevent reels of machine embroidery thread from becoming entangled with each other is to wrap them individually in plastic wrap. You can still see the colors but won't get a bird's nest!

I feel about threads the way a painter cherishes certain paints. Those I recommend are the ones I use in my particular type of work, but there is an infinite range of threads on the market, designed for machine and hand embroidery, sewing and quilting, plus fancy yarns of all descriptions, and every embroiderer tends to have his or her own favourites.

For hand embroidery, especially *shisha* work, I use rayon thread almost exclusively, particularly DMC, which comes in a very large and subtle range of shades. I also find that the colours and the texture of this yarn are very close to Indian colours, which range from vibrant shades to subtle ones that may not at first sight appear terribly interesting, but that come to life when put next to a brilliant colour. Anchor's Marlitt is also rayon, but the colour range is more limited and less subtle. Another splendid yarn is produced by De Haviland (see list of suppliers on page 127). This comes in luscious individually-dyed hanks, some plain, some variegated. The yarn can also be dyed to individual requirements. It is rayon, but it has almost the feel and texture of floss silk, which is extremely hard to find, even in India. The only drawback to rayon thread is that it is slippery. It rarely tangles, which is a plus point, but unless the beginnings and ends of your work are well secured the thread will start unravelling. Natesh is an Indian brand of threads, and the range includes attractive machine embroidery rayon yarns in wonderful colours.

I rarely use stranded cotton. I find that it does not 'spread' sufficiently for *shisha* work or *kantha* quilting, and it tends to knot. I occasionally use it for feather, buttonhole or chain stitch embroidery. Again, I tend to prefer the DMC colours, as I find them more subtle and closer to Indian hues.

I use a lot of metallic threads, both for hand and machine embroidery. For hand work, I choose DMC perlé metallic, which comes in a range of silvers and golds, and also in metallic colours. I like contrasting it with the softer sheen of the rayon thread (see the *shisha* work on *Crooked Paths*, page 108). I am also partial to the Madeira version, which I use doubled for hand work. This thread can also be wound round the bobbin and used in machine embroidery, but it is too thick to put through the machine needle.

For machine embroidery proper, I again love rayon threads – both Madeira and Natesh produce brilliant as well as subtle shades. The thread is strong and rarely breaks on the machine, provided the upper tension is adjusted properly (the same applies to metallic threads). Güttermann threads are especially good, although thicker than Madeira. Used side by side, these two create subtle textural contrasts.

I also use pure silk thread in machine embroidery. Imported from Japan, it is expensive, but very beautiful.

I tend to use pure cotton for the bobbin thread, in conjunction with machine embroidery thread. Güttermann threads are excellent for this and, of course, for hand and machine plain sewing. The colour is more or less irrelevant. If the tension is correctly adjusted, the under thread should not show on top. Sometimes, however, an interesting effect can be achieved by allowing the bottom thread to show slightly on the top of the work. In this case, select a pure cotton thread a few tones darker or lighter than the upper embroidery thread. I used this effect in *The Sea, the Sea* on page 106.

I work almost exclusively with silk fabrics laid over a fine cotton lawn foundation, and I find that for plain sewing, whether by hand or machine, plain cotton or polyester Güttermann threads are best. Never be tempted to buy unknown threads from the bargain bin. They may be prone to breakage and knotting.

Monofilament thread resembles an ultra-fine fishing line and is useful when sewing over fabrics of many different colours, as it saves you having to change colour all the time. Use the clear variety over pale colours and the smoky over darker shades. A good tip is to touch the end of the thread with a black marker to render it easier to thread through the eye of the needle.

For hand quilting, there is a range of pre-waxed cotton threads, which are strong and do not knot. I especially like the Güttermann version. Remember that quilting thread should never be used on the machine, as the coating could clog the works. For hand and machine quilting, I also tend to use pure cotton thread. I keep a wax dispenser close at hand when I hand-quilt, to prevent the thread from knotting. For machine quilting I also use rayon and metallic machine embroidery threads, and occasionally polyester thread.

There is also a huge range of decorative threads available for hand embroidery. Mohair wool and cotton chenille, for example, can be couched and mixed with beautiful Japanese or other gold threads.

Delicate embroidery silk ribbon is not a thread, of course, yet it belongs in this section as it is used to hand-embroider. It is particularly effective for daisy stitch and French knots.

The Sewing Machine

A cursory glance through this book will have shown you that I love mixing free-motion machine embroidery with hand work. Technically speaking, free-motion embroidery can be produced with the simplest of electric domestic sewing machines, provided it has a zigzag stitch. Yet you may wish to invest in an up-to-date model. I am a relative latecomer to machine embroidery, since my old sewing machine did much to discourage me from investigating the potentials of this fascinating range of techniques. Although described as 'portable', it was so heavy that bringing it out of its cupboard always seemed too much of an effort. Buying a sensibly priced modern lightweight machine hastened my conversion and opened up all manner of new vistas.

Nowadays all good electric sewing machines come with a zigzag stitch, and almost all of them offer a range of additional stitches. Machine manufacturers have developed automatic stitches that are an extension of the zigzag stitch, and some machines are computerized and can be programmed to work a chosen design or retain a particular pattern in their memory. There is, however, no real need to have a huge repertoire of automatic stitches. I only use two with any frequency in my work: satin and fagotting stitches. The rest are all created with free-motion embroidery.

When the machine is used for ordinary sewing purposes, the feed dogs are up, moving up and down in a rolling motion, pulling the fabric under the needle and setting the length of each stitch. For free-motion machine embroidery; you need, in effect, to disable the automatic functions of the machine. Depending on your machine, the feed dogs must either be lowered, usually by pressing a button, or covered with a darning plate. The foot is removed altogether or replaced by a special darning foot. It is difficult to be precise as each machine works in a different way. The only way to get to grips with the capabilities of your own machine is to study the manual in detail. Some shops offer basic courses to purchasers, or at least have helpful staff prepared to answer queries. You should find a reference to free-machine embroidery in your manual; it is sometimes described as 'darning', but the basic technique is the same. Once the feed dogs are lowered or covered up, the fabric is no longer fed automatically through the machine, which allows the embroiderer to move it up and down or sideways, and to control the length of the stitches.

The other point to consider when purchasing your machine is that you should be able to adjust the tension. Some manufacturers advise against this, but it is essential for embroidery. The top tension is adjusted by turning the dial or knob, which is usually marked from 0 to 10. Normal tension ranges between 3 to 5; 6 to 10 will be very tight. In normal sewing, the golden rule is that the upper and lower tensions should be perfectly balanced. This may not apply to machine embroidery, as only the upper part of the work will normally be seen and it therefore does not matter if the top thread shows slightly on the underside of the work. Choose a machine with an easily removable bobbin case. The tension in the bobbin may also need adjusting. This is done by holding the bobbin case with the side where the thread is inserted towards you, then turning the tension screw clockwise to increase tension or anticlockwise to decrease it. Only give one half-turn adjustment at a time, and take great care that the tiny screw does not pop out and get lost. I tend to keep a couple of bobbin cases adjusted for low tension, marking them accordingly with a dab of nail varnish, while keeping an 'untouched' case for straight sewing. For free-motion embroidery, it is preferable to use a machine with a flat bed, as a sloping one may interfere with the movement of the embroidery frame.

Feet and attachments

Most machines come with a set of accessories, some of which are very useful for embroidery. The open-toe embroidery foot is a must for satin-stitch embroidery. Look for one with a wide groove on the underside to allow thick or wide stitching to go through unimpeded. I find the ones made of clear plastic especially good, as they allow you to see the work as you stitch. Quilting feet come in a variety of sizes and you'll need to find the type best adapted to your machine. As mentioned before, the foot is often removed altogether when preparing the machine for free-motion embroidery; some models, however, can take or require a darning foot to assist in stabilizing the fabric during free-motion machine embroidery. The foot also protects the fingers from the exposed needle. Here again, you must consult the manual or the suppliers of your machine. A piping foot is also handy when attaching zips or piping around a cushion.

Embroidery frames

Frames for hand embroidery may be made of plastic, wood or metal. The best ones have an open outer ring, which is tightened with a screw. I personally prefer wooden rings. Before using them, especially when embroidering on silks and delicate fabrics, the inner ring must be wound tightly with a cotton tape, secured with a few stitches. This will prevent the wood from snagging the fabric as it is tightened.

A frame is an absolute necessity for free-motion machine embroidery, in order to keep the fabric taut as you move it under the needle. My preference is for the plastic type with a groove on the inner side of the ring, into which fits a springy metal ring. These are the best adapted for working with the delicate fabrics that I use. The diameter should be between 12 and 16 cm/5 and 6$^1/_2$ in maximum, to ensure that the fabric held in the ring makes close contact with the needle plate. (A frame made for hand embroidery is generally too high to pass under the presser bar of modern machines.)

Needles

Hand-embroidery needles have longer eyes than those used for plain sewing, and are graded in sizes from fine (high numbers) to coarse (low numbers). Because I work on such a variety of fabrics, it is difficult to give exact indications as to sizes. My rule is to try to use as fine a needle as will allow the thread to pass comfortably through the eye (if the hole is too small it will cause the thread to fray and break). You will soon find a couple of sizes you feel happy with and stick to them. For hand quilting, there are special short, somewhat stubby, needles. A glance through this book will show that the projects involve a good deal of straight hand sewing and, here again, fine needles are best for stitching through silk and cotton lawn. Remember that needles do not last for ever. Change them frequently, before the point becomes blunt or the hole sharp, causing the thread to fray and break.

Machine needles come in sizes ranging from 8 to 20 (US and British) or 60 to 120 (continental), the lower numbers being very fine and the high numbers coarser. There are also special embroidery needles with a larger hole than normal, and these are particularly useful for metallic threads, which are often prone to fraying. The size required also depends on the embroidery surface. Have a range of embroidery needles to hand, and experiment on a piece of the selected fabric, using the actual thread, to decide which is best. Top-stitching needles are extra sharp and have a very long eye. They can take much heavier thread than ordinary needles, and can even take two threads. Because of the large eye, they tend to break more easily, but some embroiderers find them useful for metallic embroidery threads or for quilting. Special quilting needles are also available. Both free-motion embroidery and machine quilting put great stress on needles and you should remember to change them frequently. Singer and Schmetz make excellent specialist needles which have a coloured band on the shaft to indicate their purpose. This feature makes them easy to identify when they are out of the box.

Other equipment

You will need a good pair of dressmaker's scissors for general fabric cutting, and small, pointed embroidery scissors. (I also have a pair on a chatelaine which I hang around my neck – invaluable, as small scissors invariably vanish on the table when one is working on a large piece.) You will also require a wax dispenser, through which a length of sewing or quilting thread can be passed to prevent knotting, a seam ripper to unpick stitches without damaging the fabric, well-fitting thimbles and a large box of extra long, fine steel pins. Accessories for marking out patchwork and quilting fabrics include white and silver quilting pencils, a long steel ruler, a short one with a marker that can be set to a chosen width (very useful to mark seam or border widths), a rotary cutter and a plastic cutting mat.

As a lot of my work involves patchwork, it is important to have a hot steam iron on the go all the time. Check that the steam passages are clear and that the water really comes out as steam. Droplets are a problem when working with silks, as they often leave marks that are impossible to remove without washing the fabric. I also keep a can of spray starch handy and use it in the preparation of the fabric (see paragraph on cotton lawn, page 25). Here, too, make sure to give the can a good shake and check that the starch comes out as a really fine spray over the silk.

Finally, it is vital to stress the importance of working at a table of an appropriate height while sitting correctly. Your feet should comfortably rest on the floor and you may find it helpful to use a footstool when hand embroidering. The same applies to working at the sewing machine. Make sure the table is the right height so as to avoid tension in the neck and shoulder muscles. For me, embroidery is so addictive and absorbing that I find it difficult to stop when I am involved in a piece. Remember to get up every couple of hours, shake your shoulders and take a few steps around the room to relax the muscles and ensure good blood circulation. Good natural or artificial light is vital. I unavoidably and frequently end up working at night, and a daylight bulb is an invaluable aid when judging colours. Silk is especially treacherous, as the colour can look entirely different in daylight. When I plan a piece – especially crazy patchwork – I always try to look at the colour arrangement in daylight and in normal electric light. This gives me an idea of the final result in a domestic setting, where it will have to look its best by day and by night.

Above and below. Details from Summer Fever, *see page 77.*

Fabrics

Silk My great love is silk. This is my fabric of choice, whether as a base for pieces that are pure embroidery, such as *Leafy Trail* (see page 110), or to create tumbling blocks (see *Adrift*, on page 105), or indeed for the patches of a crazy patchwork, as on page 77. In crazy patchwork, I frequently introduce materials ranging from antique lace to velvet, linen, pure cotton and even woollens to create a richly textured surface. Very occasionally, I will include a few scraps of man-made fabric, but they have to be truly exceptional! I have hoarded fabrics all my life, and wherever I travel I look for interesting materials to bring back. If you have the opportunity to travel to India, ask the hotel to recommend a good shop. Sari shops tend to store silks and fine cottons in an incredible range of shades as they are used to make the blouses which Indian women wear under the sari. As these have to be matched exactly, it is possible to buy a selection of reds ranging from off-white to the deepest shades of crimson and so on for all the colours of the rainbow. Raw silks and tussores come in many different weights and textures, and shot silks can lend a unique richness to your work. Also look for those wonderfully textured silks produced for men's *kurtas,* which are loose-fitting shirts, as well as for thick and velvety *matka* silks, strong and closely woven spun silks, and beautiful wood-block printed silks. These can be bought on the bolt, and are designed for the *shalwar kurta,* which is the smart trouser and top outfit worn by young girls and women. There is something in me that weeps when I see a sari being cut up, unless it is old and can be recycled. Look for the lengths of old sari borders that are sold in certain shops. You will also find an infinite variety of natural/man-made fabrics that are not made in the west and by and large not exported: silk and cotton, rayon and cotton, pure rayon and many other permutations, many of which are both stunning and very good value.

Few people realize how diverse and versatile silk fibres can be. Silk weaves range from an absolute gossamer, to the most incredibly tightly-woven fine and yet very tough fabrics (parachutes were once made of pure silk!), including suit- and coat-weight materials. It is, of course, a costly fabric, but the great advantage of being an embroiderer is that a tiny quantity of a very expensive fabric will go a long way and impart life and richness to cheaper neighbours. Find out who is the best supplier of silks in your home town and ask when their seasonal sale of remnants takes place. This is the time to stock up! You may also wish to recycle fabrics. I tend to avoid this on conservation grounds, unless they are genuine antique fabrics. I will then use them in small quantities and back them with fine cotton lawn to reinforce them.

If you are adept at dyeing or printing on cloth, buy plain silks and dye or print them to your required colours. Tea can be excellent when you want delicately shaded silks ranging in colour from cream to tobacco. I used this method for some of the fabrics in the cathedral window panel of *Winter Days*, on page 81. Make a strong tea liquor, and pour it into three or four containers. Leave the first one neat and dilute the others to an increasing degree to obtain lighter shades. Steep the silk in the containers; leave for at least thirty minutes, and rinse, first in salt water and then in clear. Allow the fabrics to drip-dry, and then press them. You should end up with a delicately graded range of sepia-coloured silks. The same method can also be used to tone down a printed fabric that may look a little too bright or new, when used with recycled materials. In this case, use a medium-strength concoction and leave the fabric in it for from 15 to 20 minutes only.

Fine cotton lawn This is a fabric that I use in industrial quantities. When I prepare a piece of silk as the background to embroidery, as in *Leafy Trail*, on page 110, for example, I cut a piece of cotton lawn to the same size; press both fabrics; spray them lightly with starch and press them together. This makes them adhere to each other and I can then stay-stitch and zigzag the edges. After this, to all intents and purposes they form a single fabric which will not fray (always a problem with silk) and is ready to be embroidered. I also use this fine cotton lawn as the foundation cloth for crazy patchwork and as a backing for many pieces.

Domett This is a cotton flannel and unless otherwise specified, I use it as an interlining. It comes in a variety of weights, and I use the type sold as curtain interlining. This is soft, heavy and stable, and it gives a wonderful body to a long narrow piece, such as *Crooked Paths* on page 108.

Polyester batting/wadding For pieces with a highly sculptured surface, such as the crazy patchwork pieces, *Summer Sprites* on page 85 or *Dawn Blooms* on page 93, I use polyester batting/wadding. This comes in a variety of thicknesses (loft), and I generally select the lightweight variety.

Fusible interfacing Iron-on interfacing can be useful to give body to a flimsy silk. Always read the manufacturer's instructions.

Fusible webbing This material has a heat-sensitive agent applied to a paper backing and is useful for bonding one material to another, for example, when appliquéing. Bondaweb (UK), made by Vilene, is sold in the US under the name of Wonder-Under and of Vliesofix in Europe. This is the type I prefer, and I have used it for pieces such as *Night Blooms* (see pages 94–95) and for the Kandinski pictures (see pages 53 and 123).

Overleaf. Detail from Mellow Fruitfulness. *See complete piece on page 79.*

HAND EMBROIDERY

Mirror Work – *Shisha*

For many westerners *shisha* work – sadly often the inferior examples destined for the tourist trade – has become synonymous with Indian embroidery. It is true that it is peculiar to India, starting first as a courtly pastime and then being adopted by village women, especially in Gujarat and Kutch and spreading to Rajasthan and the Deccan.

Shisha work is said to have been developed at the Moghal court by the beautiful Mumtaz Begum, the wife of Shah Jahan, who built the Taj Mahal in her memory at Agra in the middle of the seventeenth century. The popularity of this type of embroidery coincided with the development of glass making in India, in a process using sand, lime and soda in small furnaces. As in the west, glass and mirrors were regarded as a great luxury, and they were used in princely houses only. In India, entire rooms can still be found in which every available inch of wall and ornate ceiling is covered with mirror fragments, embedded in plaster. These reception rooms were often used for private dance entertainments, the beautiful dancer's colourful garments and rich jewellery reflected endlessly all over the room. As glass-making processes improved, glass became cheaper. The glass was blown into large spheres; the back would be silvered to produce a mirror, and the surface was then cut up with special cutters, shaped like loosely hinged scissors. The resulting *shishas* tended to be slightly convex, and examining them and the quality of the real silver or gold thread used in the embroidery is one of the ways to date antique Indian textiles. The little mirror pieces became available to village and nomad women, who bought them from peddlers at village fairs. The women incorporated the *shishas* into the colourful embroidery with which they covered their clothing, and also made them into decorative or religious hangings for their homes (in India there is no real dividing line between the religious and the secular).

As mentioned in the introduction to this book, mirrors are regarded as auspicious and are reputed to afford the wearer protection against the evil eye. It is still common in the villages of Gujarat and Rajasthan to see a small child wearing a hat or carrying a small bag studded with mirror work. Almost invariably, the child will also have a dab of kohl in some odd place on its face, left there by its loving mother after applying kohl around its eyes. Kohl, prepared from lamp black, and applied around the eyes as a beauty aid by women, and now less frequently by men, is also put around children's eyes, even those of tiny babies, as it is ascribed therapeutic properties beneficial to the eye. The idea is to bring out the beauty of the child's eyes and keep them healthy, but such a perfectly handsome child being a temptation to destiny, a black mark on its cheek makes it less perfect and may ward off the evil eye!

Opposite page. Fine example of antique shisha *work, integrated into a rich floral pattern.*

Shisha embroidery is produced by women in villages. Many have formed themselves into cooperatives; the cooperative supplies its members with raw materials and design suggestions, and buys up the products of their industry to sell to city dwellers in India and to the export market. The fact that this type of work is now enjoying a great revival of interest and appreciation in India, as well as abroad, has opened up new vistas for these women. A craft they once used for utilitarian purposes, as well as a rare diversion from the never-ending round of work on the land, the preparation of meals and the care of children, has in recent years become a quite significant source of income, which has subtly altered the economic balance between men and women at village level in those areas. Women now have an area of influence that is strictly their own, and access to money that they can spend on their daughters or in purchasing stoves and other things to make their daily life less of a drudgery. The cooperatives often act as a support system for the women: the members pay regular small amounts to the common pot and after a while can take their turn to draw out this money for well-needed purchases or to cope with family debts or illnesses. I was delighted to observe a similar phenomenon during a fascinating journey through the uplands of the state of Chiapas, in Mexico, a couple of years back. Still surviving in the mountains are Mayan villages, in which people have retained their own languages, and sometimes, but not always, speaking Spanish as well. These people are the direct descendants of the builders of the Palenque and Chichén Itzá temple and palace complexes. The women produce amazing weavings which now sell for high prices abroad. While their husbands traditionally eke out a precarious living, working as seasonal labourers on coffee plantations or in forestry, the women, who traditionally had very little say in family or village affairs, now enjoy a measure of economic independence, and there, too, it will not be easy to put the genie back in the bottle!

Coming back to *shishas,* these are cut in a variety of shapes – round, triangular or square – and can vary in size from the minute to the very large. They are sometimes made of tin, especially when used in the large colourful cotton awnings that are hung from the ceiling over a verandah, for instance, to protect the sitters from the sun, or as a bed canopy. Such pieces are often produced by the women of the nomadic tribes that still roam the countryside and the city streets of Rajasthan, working as street performers or hiring themselves as casual labour in villages. The embroideries they produce are vividly coloured, with large floral motifs, stylized birds and animals that form part of the daily scene – cows, horses, camels, monkeys, peacocks and hens.

This desire to surround oneself with bright colours on clothing or home accessories seems indelibly linked to the arid landscape of Rajasthan, parts of which are desert. Travelling through the state, it is fascinating to watch the women working in the fields.

Their skirts of thick cotton are still often covered with intricate embroidery. They wear a tight-fitting blouse, the *choli,* under their veil, and this blouse is often completely covered with *shishas.* The veil – *odhni* – is pulled well over the face, hiding it from prying eyes, but also as a protection from the implacable sun. The embroidery is a form of darning as well as a source of decoration – a tear in the skirt means another patch (not always matching), soon covered with a colourful motif.

If you visit India and are looking for textiles to buy, do not automatically aim for the cheapest. Tourist goods, as tends to happen in many parts of the world, depreciate the really fine work produced by embroiderers and other artisans. Take a little time to compare. Look at the materials used, the size of the stitches, and the care and thought that has gone into the design and working of the piece. The rate of exchange is so much weighted in your favor that a few extra pounds or dollars can make the difference between acquiring shoddy goods or something that is a minor work of art. It is also by buying the products of real artisans and enabling them to make a reasonable living that their craftsmanship can be encouraged and passed on to future generations. It is all too easy to blame people for selling poorly designed or badly finished articles while ignoring the fact that they are being asked to work incredibly long hours for a ludicrous wage. Food for thought! The practice of replacing the embroidery that attaches the *shisha* by small metal rings, already wrapped with a crudely-coloured machine buttonhole stitch, is a good example of what I mean. The ring is put over the *shisha* and fixed to the cloth with a few stitches. Modern embroiderers in India sometimes fix *shishas* by means of a tambour hook, and they have now evolved a way of fixing them with machine embroidery. It gives an interesting effect and has been used successfully by many people, but I do not use this technique.

As will be immediately obvious when leafing through this book, I use *shishas* extensively, but contrary to the traditional usage, in which they form part of a repeat pattern, I scatter them freely. They often form the starting point of a piece of work, anchoring the rest of the embroidery, creating focal points and defining the colour scheme. I always use round, medium-sized *shishas* (approximately 1 cm/½ in in diameter). I have on occasion used tiny ones, but the smaller the *shisha,* the more fiddly the embroidery! (You will find the address of a reliable mail-order supplier at the end of this book.) I usually start out by scattering and arranging the *shishas* over the cloth, and tracing lightly around them with a quilting pencil, to mark their eventual location. Most of my hand embroidery is made with two strands of DMC rayon thread, but it is fun to try out different yarns, such as DMC perlé metallic, Natesh floss silk or stranded cotton. The latter is fine, but tends to knot. It is interesting,

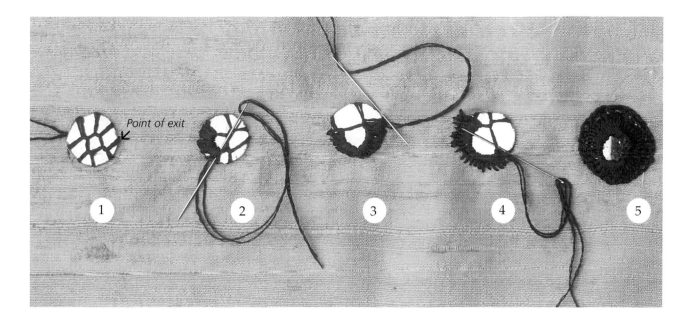

Point of exit

1   2   3   4   5

however, to contrast its matt texture with the shiny yarns mentioned earlier. I have even experimented with mohair. The mirror seen through the hairy texture creates an interesting effect.

There are many different ways of attaching *shishas*, and each embroiderer will have her or his favourite way of doing it. The golden rule, however, is to put the thumb firmly over the *shisha*, holding it in position and not moving the thumb until the base stitches are completed. The first step is to make two vertical stitches, followed by two horizontal ones, weaving the thread round the verticals. The thread must be drawn firmly, as the holding stitches will get pulled out towards the edges of the mirror by the top stitching. If they are loose, the *shisha* may fall out. Bring the needle to the front of the work in the opposite direction from the point of exit (see 1 above). The *shisha* is now secure and you can decide which stitch to use to embroider round it. With practice you will soon discover your own favourite method and also decide how close you want to have the basic stitches, as this determines how much of the actual *shisha* is visible after working the decorative stitch around it.

The stitches I chiefly use are *shisha* and a sort of herringbone, each of which produces a slightly different effect (see 2 to 4 above). I then invariably work a row of chain stitch around the *shisha* (see 5 above) and I may leave it at this or add a row of buttonhole stitches (see detail on page 61, for example). I may even turn the *shisha* into a motif. On pages 43–44 you will find a series of simple designs, based on Indian motifs which I have used on crazy patchwork (see *Winter Days*, on page 81, for instance).

1. The holding stitches.

2. Second step. The shisha *stitch. The needle is inserted under the holding threads. Hold the thread under the needle and pull tight.*

3. Third step. Take a tiny stitch into the fabric, close to the edge of the circle. Loop the thread under the needle and draw tight. Repeat second step.

4. This is a variation on the shisha *stitch. The needle takes a small vertical stitch close to the circle, the needle is inserted under the holding stitches and over the thread more or less as for a herringbone stitch.*

5. The shisha *worked as in stage 4 is framed by a row of chain stitch.*

Other Hand Embroidery Stitches

The sampler on the right shows the stitches I commonly use in my work. Most of them will already be familiar to you. Please note that Indian embroiderers tend to work away from themselves, while you're probably used to directing the stitches towards you. Simply use the method you feel most comfortable with; the result will be the same.

1 **Chain stitch** This stitch is very ancient and appears to have been used in many different parts of the world. In India, it is used both for outlining and for filling shapes. Fabrics from Kashmir are often entirely covered with motifs and backgrounds worked entirely in chain stitch. This type of embroidery is generally worked over a frame, using a tambour hook for speed. I use the hand method for this stitch, usually as a surround to *shishas*. Keep the thread tension and the size of the loops even. Make sure that the needle is always inserted into the centre of the previously made loop, in order to produce the next.

2 **Bi-coloured chain stitch** This is made in exactly the same way as normal chain stitch, but using two strands of thread of different colours. One loop is made, catching the first (red) thread with the needle, while the second colour is held above the work. The next loop uses the second colour, while the first thread is kept out of the way. Keep your thread lengths reasonably short to prevent knots. This is a very effective stitch with which to fill in shapes, as multiple rows create interesting effects, see 2a, opposite.

3 **Stem stitch** This is useful for outlines, flower stems and so on.

4, 4a **Feather stitch and double feather stitch** This stitch, which can also be tripled, was traditionally used to decorate the edges of crazy patchwork (see *Indian Spring Memories* on page 68).

5 **Buttonhole stitch** The stitches can be worked open, as shown, or set close together. In India, buttonhole is often used in parallel rows to fill motifs (see 5a opposite and motif 1 on page 44). When working in rows, it is important to begin each new row by inserting the needle into the previous loop.

6 **Daisy stitch** I use these little flowers a lot in clumps on a crazy patchwork background, see page 35. The stitch is exactly like a chain stitch loop. A small straight stitch is then made on the top to attach the loop to the cloth. Once the eight petals of the flower are completed, I usually work a second and shorter loop inside the finished petal, see 6a, and put one or more beads at the centre of each flower. I also work these daisies around *shishas*, but of course you'll need many more petals for this. To position them neatly,

Opposite page. The sampler shows a selection of the hand stitches that I commonly use in my work.

imagine that the flower is a clock; put petals at 12, 3, 6 and 9 o'clock, then insert petals between each, and repeat the process. The base of the petals can be covered with beading (see sketch 3 on page 44).

7 **French knots** Pick up a tiny amount of cloth with the needle and wrap the thread three or four times around the needle, depending on the size of knot required. Use your thumb-nail to hold the loops on the needle. Do not tighten the thread too much, but it must be taut. Keep the length fairly short to help prevent the thread from knotting as you pull the needle through the loops. Stitch 7a shows a loop made by twisting the thread fourteen times around the needle. These larger loops are used in the making of rosettes, see 7b. Several loops are worked next to each other, but at slightly different angles, until a pleasing shape is obtained. For an example, see the detail of *Winter Days*, on the frontispiece page, in which I wanted bright little dabs of red to suggest the berries that brighten up the dark winter landscape. These were made up of rosettes of French knots.

8 **Spiders** Work two stitches of the desired length to form a cross. The needle is brought to the centre and turned around so that you insert the blunt end of the needle (with the eye) under and around each leg of the spider, keeping the thread gently taut, see 8a. Work all the way around until the spider forms a convex shape above the cloth, see 8b. Always make sure that you have enough thread in the needle to complete the spider.

9 **Herringbone stitch** This, too, was often used to outline the patches of crazy patchwork. It can be worked quite open or with the legs close together, looking almost like an elongated cross stitch. In India, multiple rows of this stitch, positioned very close together, are often used as a filling stitch.

10 *Rabari tanka* This popular Indian stitch is used extensively to fill in shapes such as the small mango or paisley shape on the sampler (see 10 on previous page). It is a sort of double chain stitch. It is important to insert the needle through the previous loop, keeping the loop slightly open with your thumb. Keep the tension even and loop the thread alternately to the left and right to form a double row of chain stitches (see left).

11, 12, 13 and 14 These are all filling stitches that I use extensively (see the background of *Serenity*, on page 114, and the detail opposite).

15, 15a, 15b and 15c Running or darning stitch These are examples of running stitches, as used in *kantha* quilting (see next section).

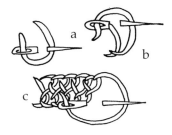

Opposite. A detail from Summer Fever, which displays a variety of filling, or speckling, stitches.

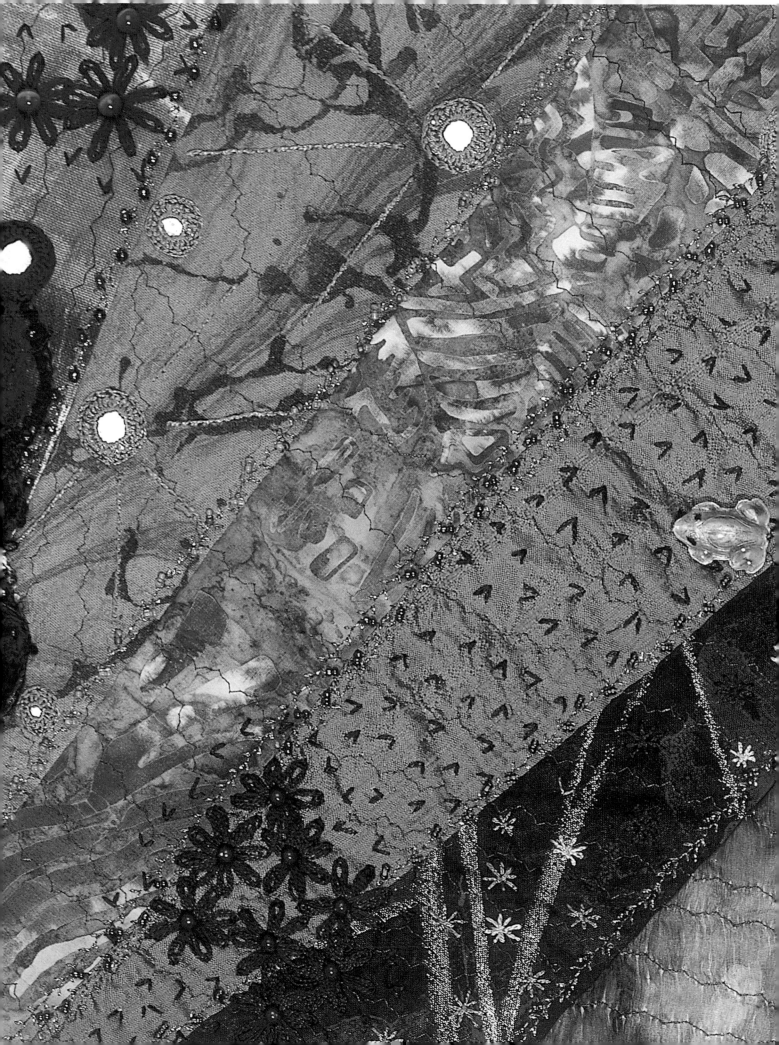

Kantha and other Quilting Traditions around the World

Quilting is practically a universal tradition, in which two or three layers of fabric are held together to produce a warm, possibly highly decorative, covering. It was often a rural activity, dictated by the necessity to 'make do and mend'. In seventeenth-century England, there were fine traditions of quilting as well as of patchwork, which settlers took with them to the United States. There they met with other ethnic groups, who brought their own traditions of fine needlework. In the early years of a pioneer family's life, conditions in a sod house or a log cabin were often harsh and extremely cold, and new supplies hard to come by. It was imperative for the family to live off its resources and recycle anything that could be used. Worn-out clothing, calico flour sacks and other unpromising materials were hoarded to be worked into quilts. Some pieces, such as memorial quilts, are pitiful reminders of the harshness of life. They were often made of patches saved from dead relatives' clothing, their dates of birth and death carefully recorded on the patches with Indian ink.

Apart from these somewhat sad reminders of human suffering, other early examples of pioneer quilts have survived, made of unbleached and red calico fabrics, and the intricacy of the piecing has made these into genuine works of art. It is obvious how much the women who made some of these pieces enjoyed and derived pride from their talent. As pioneer communities developed into settlements and towns, cabinet-makers and shops selling an increasing range of goods enabled these women to create the homes they had dreamed about and gave them more leisure hours to spend on their quilts. Quilt-making became an essential part of the social life of women, and the members of quilting bees vied with each other to demonstrate their inventiveness and the extent of their repertoire.

It is really in the United States that the quilt as an art form was born. New England, where the early European settlers had first arrived, quickly became a by-word for elegance and sophistication. The ladies who worked on their quilts in the drawing rooms of Boston were lunar miles removed from the humble pioneer wives trying to make a living in the wilds of Montana or Oregon. The Boston Album quilts, made of rich fabrics and evermore intricate piecing, had little to do with keeping the cold at bay, but provided their makers with a truly artistic form of expression. Young women were expected to enter marriage with a collection of fine quilts, utilitarian as well as decorative. The mother and the sisters of the bride would make a special wedding quilt, incorporating the famous double-ring motif, to be given to the young couple on their wedding day.

Opposite page. A dharaniyo, a cover for a pile of quilts. This is an early 20th-century piece from an aristocratic household in Gujarat.

Even the Mennonite Christian communities, who had come to Pennsylvania from Switzerland and Germany to escape religious persecution in the middle of the seventeenth century, and who lived according to a very strict moral code that discouraged ornament of any kind, developed a style of quilt-making that is truly stunning. The Amish, who broke away from the Mennonites in the eighteenth century, describe themselves as 'the plain people'. They used – and often still use – a limited palette of plain fabrics, woven from fine wool rather than cotton, and never silks or other 'showy' fabrics, yet they produced quilts that look like early abstract paintings: diamonds in the square, simple bars and plain borders, all simplicity and elegance. Glowing, often dark, colours are placed in unexpected juxtapositions that give them a unique beauty. No clever piecing here – but wonderfully fine and intricate quilting. Myriads of tiny hand stitches, perfectly regular, worked tone on tone, sculpting the surface of the quilts. I discovered these quilts many years ago, and although my own work can appear the very antithesis of this study in simplicity, I feel a real affinity with these women and these people so concerned with maintaining their culture and way of life in an increasingly global world.

In India too, quilting is highly popular, both as a way of recycling worn-out fabrics and saris, but also as a folk art. In Northern India, where the winter nights can be bitterly cold, the *rezai* or quilt was introduced by the Muslims in the sixteenth century and remains a popular bed covering. Several *rezai* still form part of a bride's dowry. Some are lightweight, and may consist of two layers of fine cotton, decorated with woodblock prints. They are easy to wash, and for warmth and loft they sometimes contain a thin layer of kapok, the soft silky fibre obtained from the silk-cotton tree. The quilt is held together with long running stitches. Increasingly, polyester, silk or cotton batting/wadding is now used. Feathers are rarely used as a filling in India, as many Hindus object to this animal product on religious grounds, but heavyweight quilts, often covered in luxurious velvet, are also made, and these are much warmer and thicker. It is customary for these utilitarian quilts to be dismantled before the winter sets in. The covers are washed and the kapok aired and redistributed or replaced, as it quickly goes lumpy and loses its insulating qualities. In the small traditional cities and towns of Northern India, special artisans go from house to house and carry out these pre-winter tasks on the roof terrace.

Opposite page. A quilt produced by the Aami Fakir Community of the Indus delta region of Sindh in Pakistan (c 1950).

A survivor of the make-do-and-mend mentality is the custom for grandmothers to use old saris to make a tiny quilt in preparation for the birth of a child. These offerings vary greatly in quality, according to the social background of the maker and her sewing abilities.

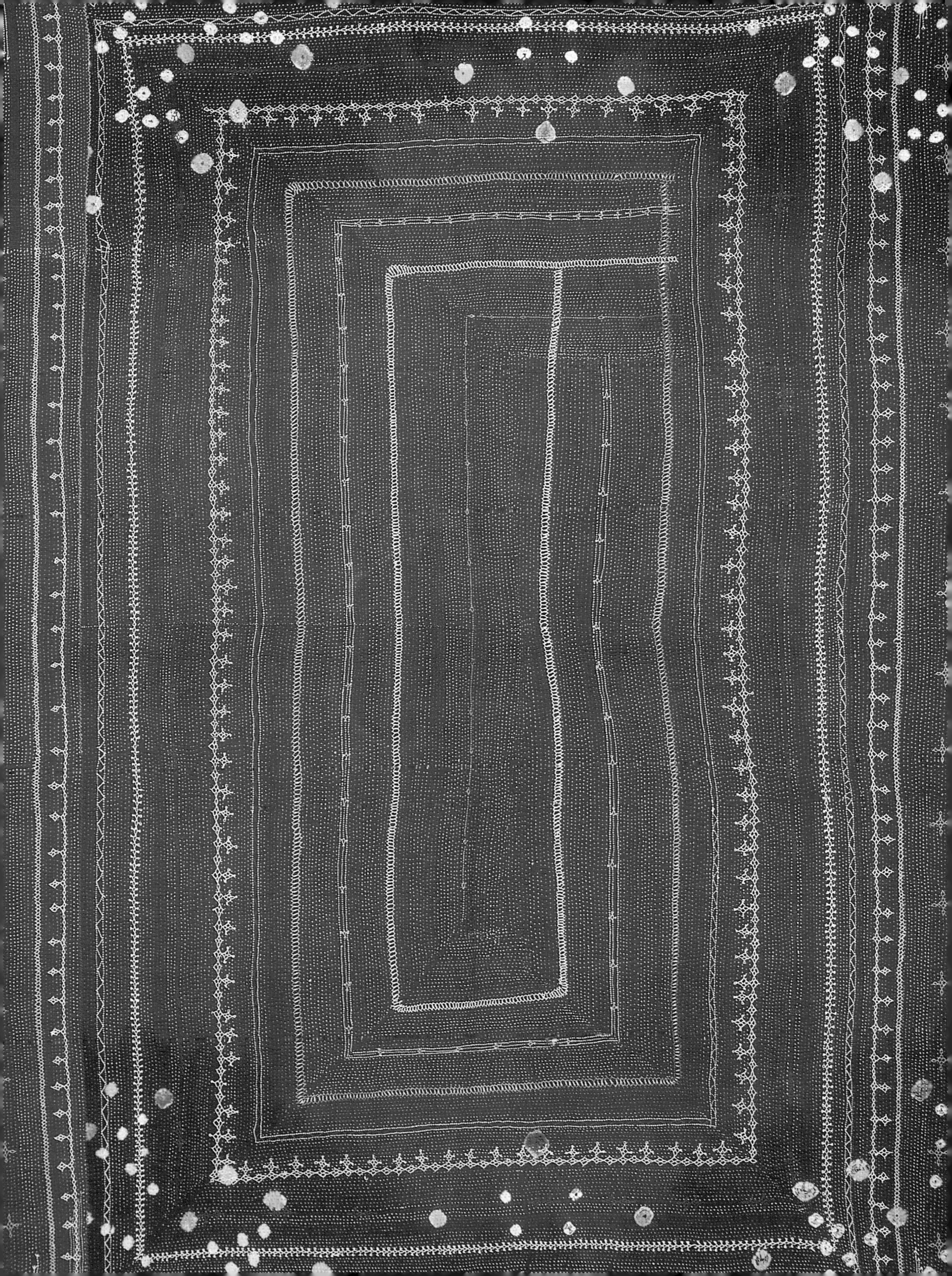

The states of Gujarat, Bihar and West Bengal have all developed distinctive traditions of quilt making that involve elaborate embroidery. Originally, these quilts would be made of re-used fabric, and it is easy to see the seams where the pieces were joined before the embroidery was added. Such quilts generally consist of two or three layers of fabric, but are rarely filled with a warm fibre. Nowadays, as in Europe and in the United States, the women cooperative workers who make these quilts rarely re-use old fabrics, as their products are designed for an increasingly appreciative urban Indian audience or for the export market. The quilts are now made to be used as bedspreads, cushions or wallhangings.

In Gujarat, the quilting may include *shisha* work and herringbone stitch, but the main body of the embroidery consists of running stitch, which in some cases is worked so that the reverse faces the maker. The finished piece is then turned over to expose the 'right' side of the work. *Kantha* quilting comes from West Bengal and from Bangladesh. This used to be a leisure activity for women, who used worn-out cotton saris and embroidered naïve animal figures, women at the well and other village scenes, as well as Radha, Krishna and other popular religious characters. The layers would be prepared and held in position with weights placed at the corners. The four sides were basted/tacked and the layers would be stitched through at regular intervals to hold them together. Close running stitches darned the pieces together so that the join between pieces was almost invisible. Traditionally, the thread used for the embroidery would be drawn out of the woven border of the sari and recycled. The maker started in the middle of the piece, working outwards. The motifs used to be embroidered from memory, but they are now more likely to be traced – alas, sometimes in leaky ballpoints. The quilt can be worked in stitches of even length, so that the back and the front of the work are the same, or with a long stitch facing the embroiderer and a short one on the other side. The background is stitched in blocks, each worked in a different direction, which gives a rippled aspect to the surface.

Now that embroiderers work on clean new cloth rather than recycled goods, *kantha* embroidery has become extremely fine, sometimes looking almost like a woven pattern. It is used as an embroidery on silk saris (see page 13 for fine examples of such work, executed in Bangladesh). The quilts are often worked on white cotton; the background stitch is also white, and colour is used for the motifs, which can be quite angular and sophisticated.

The quilts produced in Bihar are known as *sujani* and are made as bed covers. They use much the same stitches as the *kantha* pieces, but they have remained more naïve and closer to their humble folk-art origins.

Opposite. Detail of one of the blocks of Winter Days, *showing two uses of* kantha *quilting. The cream strip uses different lengths of stitch, creating a heavily incised surface that catches the light beautifully. In the grey silk strip, I used small stitches of equal length and closely aligned rows.*

I use a very simple version of *kantha* quilting in my work (see 15 and 15c, on page 33, for examples of different uses of the running stitch). Because I work exclusively on silk, I'm fascinated by the way in which this humble stitch, worked to varying lengths and spacings, can create so many different effects. The detail on the previous page is taken from *Winter Days* (see page 81). This piece contains many other examples of *kantha* quilting, some of which were worked over thick creamy duchess satin (see the bottom right-hand block, for instance).

I also like using simple circular or semi-circular shapes, which I embroider free-hand on the cloth. The detail below, taken from *Simplicity*, on page 109, is typical of this. I also used this type of embroidery in conjunction with the fine skeletons of the leaves of the *peepul* tree (see *Leafy Trail,* on page 110, and *Entrapped Leaves,* on page 112). The embroidery was, as usual, worked on two layers of fabric: the foundation lawn and the top silk fabric.

Detail from Simplicity. *The simple shapes echo each other and create a serene feeling, like a mandala.*

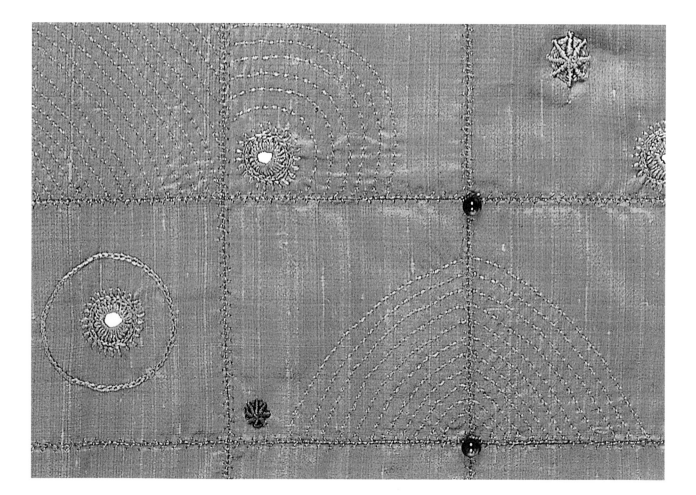

Embroidery Motifs

On the next two pages, you will find a selection of motifs. Many of these are based on traditional Indian designs, and I have used them frequently, either as they are or with slight variations, in the crazy patchwork hangings (see pages 68 to 81).

Enlarge these drawings by 200 per cent on the photocopier to use them at the same size that they have been have used in my work. Refer to the sampler on page 33 if you need to check how some of the suggested stitches are made, and also see instructions for *shisha* work, on page 31.

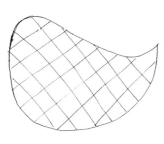

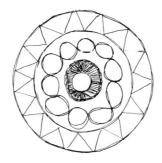

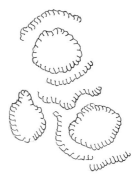

1 This is the mango, which inspired the traditional paisley design. Several of these motifs, grouped and worked in chain stitch, can be found in one of the blocks of *Summer Fever*, on page 77.

2 This motif surrounds a *shisha*, which is finished off with a row of chain stitch. The motif itself is also worked in chain stitch. You'll find several variations on the theme by leafing through this book.

3 These shapes are worked in buttonhole stitch. They are especially effective when stitched in a pale random-coloured thread.

4 A *shisha*, surrounded by a row of chain stitch, is changed into a star, worked in bi-coloured chain stitch.

5 *Shishas* here become a string of flowers. The stems are chain or stem stitch and the leaves are daisy stitch.

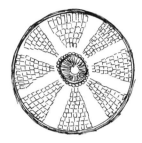

1 A *shisha* is surrounded by a traditional motif, worked in buttonhole stitch. The outer rim is made of two rows of chain stitch.

2 These double daisy-stitch flowers are also effective when worked with embroidery ribbon.

3 Beads of different sizes surround a *shisha*, completed with daisy-stitch petals; in 3a, a *shisha* is finished with a row of chain stitch, then outlined with a row of buttonhole stitch, and in 3b the *shisha* is outlined with tiny beads and surrounded by stem-stitch rays.

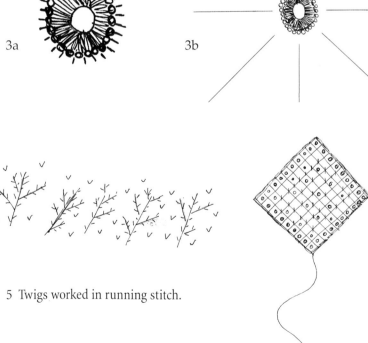

3a

3b

4 This little sprig has tiny flowers formed by rosettes of French knots. The twigs are worked in stem stitch.

5 Twigs worked in running stitch.

6 Indian children (of all ages!) are mad about kites. They fly them on hazy summer evenings from the flat roofs of houses. The gold thread was simply laid over the grid in one direction and woven under and over in the opposite direction. Small straight stitches at the intersections hold the grid in place. Pearls were attached in the squares. The tail is made of stem stitch. (See *Winter Days*, page 81, block 4.)

Other Embellishments

Couching This is a very effective technique by which thick threads, braids, ribbons and so on are applied to a surface, using hand stitchery or the zigzag stitch on the sewing machine, either with a matching or contrasting thread or a monofilament thread. The detail opposite, taken from *Winter Days*, shows how effectively silver braid can be coiled, couched and integrated into a piece of embroidery.

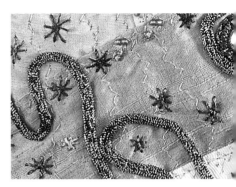

The blue detail opposite shows how a mixture of entwined yarns, including mohair wool and fine cord, can be couched and encrusted with *shishas* and beads.

 Beads of different sizes, textures and finishes (wooden, glass, pearlized and matt beads) can be clustered around a large specimen bead, as shown in the sketch on the left, and attached over a piece of couched work.

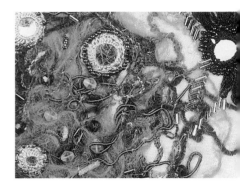

Beads, buttons and found objects I use a profusion of delicate Japanese glass embroidery beads to outline the edges of the patches in crazy patchwork pieces, scattering them among swathes of free-motion machine embroidery. I also use lots of tiny flower-shaped real mother-of-pearl buttons. Bric-à-brac shops are often treasure troves for antique buttons, costume jewellery and broken rosaries, all of which are good sources for embellishments. It is also fun to cover buttons with fabric selected to tone in with a piece of embroidery. I have used this technique in the *Summer Fever* hanging, on page 77 (see block 9 on the right). I do not like to over-use adhesive in my work and therefore tend to favour objects, such as beads, buttons and Egyptian scarabs, that I can stitch. Stitching is not always possible, however, and I use adhesive to attach fragments of abalone shell, and small Indian and Chinese coins, for luck. Feathers can be firmly stitched at the base and lightly glued along the centre vein to attach them to the fabric. I used fragile white feathers in *Winter Days* (see page 81, blocks 3 and 8), a piece in which I attempted to convey an impression of the delicate colourings and textures of a winter landscape. The eye of a beautiful peacock feather was used at the base of *Blue Window*, on page 75.

Peepul leaf skeletons I frequently incorporate these delicate and beautiful natural structures into my embroidery. At a recent exhibition, I had the greatest difficulty in convincing some visitors that these were 'real' leaves and that, yes, they were stitched to the cloth (see the note at the bottom of page 101, and also the detail of *Leafy Trail II*, opposite).

MACHINE EMBROIDERY

Free-motion Machine Embroidery

Previous spread. A series of glass paperweights and a bookmark decorated with simple machine embroidery, which was combined with shisha work, peepul leaf skeletons and beading.

Above. Detail from the machine-embroidered border of Lost Continent; see page 103 for the whole piece.

Prepare the fabric as explained in the paragraph entitled 'fine cotton lawn', on page 25. If you wish to try out the stitch and check on the required tension, make yourself a sample, large enough to fit in the embroidery frame, using the same fabric as the eventual piece and lining it with lawn.

Refer to the section dedicated to the sewing machine and its accessories on page 20 as well as the manual for your particular machine. Lower the feed dogs or cover them with a darning plate. Remove the foot or replace it with a darning foot. Insert a bobbin filled with ordinary sewing thread and thread the machine with machine embroidery thread (see section on page 18). If you are a novice, avoid metallic threads, as these are more difficult to use. Place the plastic outer ring of the embroidery frame under the cloth and press the metal inner ring over the top. This is the reverse of using a frame for hand embroidery, in which case the work sits on top of the frame, like a drum. Here, the underside of the cloth must be in direct contact with the bed of the machine. Stretch the fabric gently until it is taut.

Most free-motion machine embroidery is worked with two basic stitches: running stitch (sewing stitch) and zigzag. The result may not be markedly different, depending on how you use them. Remember that in free machine embroidery, you are in charge. You control the stitch length and direction by moving the frame, which can be done in any direction.

To start, set the stitch length and the stitch width at '0'. Insert the needle into the cloth, holding the loose ends of the thread for a few seconds as you start, and keep the machine speed low and even. Move the frame up and down and sideways to get used to the feel of the machine. Keep your fingers on the edges of the frame and well away from the moving needle, especially if you're working without a darning foot! This is a technique in which practice will pay dividends. You can work totally randomly, but on the page opposite you'll see the patterns I use most frequently. Some go back to the 1930s and 1940s when the pioneer machine embroiderer, Dorothy Benson, first evolved these patterns and gave them names. The techniques outlined opposite are far from exhaustive, but these are the ones I use.

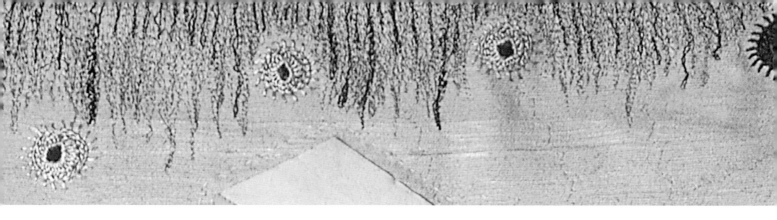

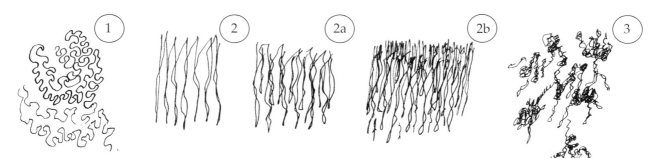

1 Crazy or vermicelli stitch consists of continuous squiggles, which can be worked at different sizes and densities. It is the most attractive background stitch and can look highly effective when surrounding motifs or negative shapes, such as the leaves in *Fragments* (see colour detail on page 100). With practice, you will learn to keep your stitches small and the curves smooth and rounded.

2 For this stitch, the frame is first moved up and down, the lines being allowed to cross and overlap. Leave spaces between the lines, as shown. The machine can be set for straight or zigzag stitch, and the sewing speed should be quite fast and even. Try using a fairly light colour for this initial row of stitches.

2a This is the second stage of the stitch. Change colour, perhaps using a gold metallic, for example, and run between the first rows of stitches. Make these lines sometimes shorter, sometimes longer than the first ones.

2b Repeat the operation, using a darker thread to fill the top of the border. The detail shown above was produced using this stitch.

3 This stitch can either be worked in a single colour or in several stages, to blend several colours. It is the closest you come to drawing with the needle. Imagine that you are holding a colour pencil or a brush, retracing your steps to make thicker lines, build up curves and put down solid areas of colour. The machine is set for straight stitch and the speed should be kept low. The embroidery detail shown on page 51 was worked in this way, as was the background to *Adrift* on page 105.

When you are working on a large area, such as the swathe of machine embroidery in the background of *Adrift* (see detail on page 61), you'll need to plan where you want the embroidery to go beforehand, and make yourself guidelines, such as hand stitches, which can easily be removed as you work. I don't trust 'erasable' pencils, especially on pale cream silk, and once the fabric is caught inside the frame, it is quite difficult to judge where you are, in relation to the other elements in the piece. For the embroidery in *Adrift*, I also used several colours. It is good practice to start with the lighter thread. Work quite sparingly at first, coming back to reinforce that colour if necessary, and then thread the machine with the second colour, keeping the metallic or the darker colour as a highlight, to be used last of all.

The same technique can be used to fill a drawn or free-hand motif, such as the blue star in *Crooked Paths,* on page 109, or the silver motif surrounding a *shisha* on page 92.

Satin stitch This stitch is worked with the feed dogs engaged, the machine being set for zigzag stitch at its closest setting and equipped with an embroidery foot with a groove on its underside (see page 20 and also refer to your machine manual). This special foot avoids 'tunnelling', which is when the cloth bunches up under the needle. The groove accommodates the thickness of the satin stitch and the fabric stays flat and smooth. When working satin stitch with a metallic thread, especially at the edge of a fabric, as for the edge of the Kandinski piece, on page 53, or the appliquéd leaf and flower, on page 94, I find it useful to work a first row of close zigzag stitches, following with the satin stitch. I make this initial row slightly narrower than the eventual satin stitch, using a yellow sewing thread under gold, or pale grey under silver. I like the edge to be really chunky and I will often work several layers of stitches until I'm satisfied with the result.

Automatic stitches Modern machines usually have a repertoire of these. I really only use the fagotting stitch, for crazy patchwork and for the grid on pieces such as *Entrapped Leaves* (see page 113). Occasionally I may select one of the fancy stitches to work randomly over crazy patches, as a preliminary to more elaborate embroideries (see detail below).

Opposite page. Detail showing the machine embroidery in the background of Night Blooms *(see pages 94–5 for the whole piece). The background was first covered with a hand-worked grid consisting of loose silver running stitch. The shishas were added, and finally free-motion machine embroidery was allowed to meander among them.*

Below. A detail taken from Mellow Fruitfulness, *showing an automatic fancy stitch worked quite randomly across the block in gold thread. This was done before starting on the hand embroidery.*

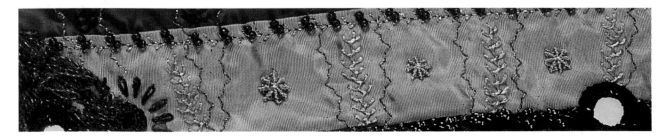

Appliqué

Homage to Kandinski, shown opposite, forms part of a series of several pictures inspired by Vassili Kandinski's works on paper. He often painted on hand-made coloured paper, using a mixture of gouache and watercolour, the first being solid and contrasting with the translucent watercolours. This created lovely effects at the points where shapes overlapped, allowing the colours to build up, as happened with the three circles on the right of my picture. I decided that appliquéd silk chiffon would give me the desired result. Discovering the strange black-and-white fabric with the elongated geometric shapes clinched it. Kandinski used to draw just such shapes very quickly with a black pen, integrating them within his watercolours. The fabric bargain counter conspiring with the spirit of the dead artist!

I used fusible webbing Vilene Bondaweb (see page 25) as the bonding agent. This has the great advantage of being colourless and translucent, which meant that it would not alter the colours of the delicate silk chiffon. The technique is described below.

1   Draw the motifs on the paper backing (smooth side) of the Bondaweb. Remember to reverse the design, unless it is asymmetrical. Cut out, leaving a margin outside the drawn lines.

2   Lay the cut pieces, adhesive side down, on the wrong side of the fabric. Using a dry iron, set to medium/wool setting (it is important to use the correct temperature), press over the paper side to transfer the adhesive from the carrier paper to the cloth. Press for three to four seconds.

3   Cut out the motifs accurately. Place them over the background fabric and choose their positions. Mark these very lightly with a quilting pencil, and then remove the paper backing. The silk chiffon pieces have to be handled delicately to prevent them from sticking to themselves.

4   Place the motifs in position on the background. Cover with a barely damp cloth and press firmly into place with the iron at the same setting as before. Press for some fifteen seconds. These instructions are for Bondaweb only. Check the manufacturer's instructions if using another brand.

I had already decided that the Kandinski pictures would be framed under glass, and the raw edges of the shapes were therefore no problem. Another picture belonging to this series appears framed on page 123.

In another piece, *Night Blooms*, on page 94, the leaves and the silver bracts of the flowers were made exactly as explained above and outlined with a wide machine satin stitch (see page 50).

The petals of the flowers in the same piece and those of *Summer Sprites*, on page 85, or of *Dawn Blooms*, on page 93, are best described as 'free standing', which means that the shapes were appliquéd over fine cotton lawn, cut out, and then outlined with satin stitch, only the base and tip of the petals being actually attached to the background of the piece. If you want to use this form of appliqué, refer to the instructions relating to the pieces mentioned, as they contain many useful tips, borne of experience.

Bondaweb, in principle, stops the cloth from fraying, although it is less effective with silk, and the edges of this material cannot really be left raw, unless for a framed piece, as explained in relation to the Kandinski pictures. If you are appliquéing closely-woven cotton or a synthetic fabric on a similar background, the edges can be left raw and, if correctly applied, the piece can be washed without problem. This method is a wonderful way to apply fun motifs on children's clothes or creating a colourful border on curtains or cushions.

Homage to Kandinski IV, 36 x 47 cm/14^{1}/$_{4}$ x 18^{1}/$_{2}$ in; its framed companion is on page 123. Photographed by Sarah Dewe.

Crazy Patchwork

I use this method extensively to create a richly textured, colourful surface on which to embroider. *Blue Window*, a detail of which appears opposite, is made of crazy patchwork, the patches being outlined with machine satin stitch, worked over a narrow black ribbon to give the illusion of stained glass. *Indian Spring Memories*, on page 69, is outlined with hand feather stitch which, with chevron stitch, was the traditional way of finishing crazy patchwork. In *Summer Fever*, on page 77, however, the patches were outlined with a machine fagotting stitch before being beaded. If you haven't used this technique before, also refer to the instructions on page 68 for *Indian Spring Memories*. The method I outline below is the one I use. There are others which you will find in specialist patchwork books.

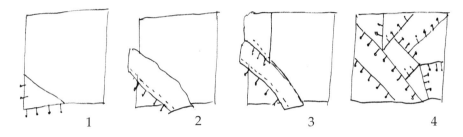

1   Make a selection of attractive fabrics and cut a square of cotton lawn; this will form the foundation of the patchwork. Cut a triangle of patchwork fabric, fix it in the corner of the square and pin it along the edges.

2   Cut a second patch. Turn and press one edge with the iron and place this over the raw edge of the triangle. This patch should extend outside the square to allow you to move it if necessary. Pin the pressed edge.

3   Repeat the process for the next patch and so on, to fill the entire square.

4   Push the raw edges of the patches under the square and look at the result carefully. Is the colour balance satisfactory? Are some of the patches too large in relation to others? Is your square too bitty or too full of violent contrasts? Remember you are preparing an embroidery surface. Will your stitches stand out? The pins allow you to move the patches or alter their shape until you are absolutely satisfied. If you are working on a large piece, comprising several blocks, prepare all the blocks up to this stage. Lay them on the floor and look at them again. Make final adjustments, and trim off the raw edges around the square. Slip-stitch the pieces and cover the edges with feather stitch. If you outline the patches with machine fagotting stitch, as I have done for most pieces, you can miss out the slip-stitching, working the decorative stitch straight over the pinned edges.

Opposite page. Detail of the top of Blue Window. *The whole piece appears on page 75.*

Cathedral Window Patchwork

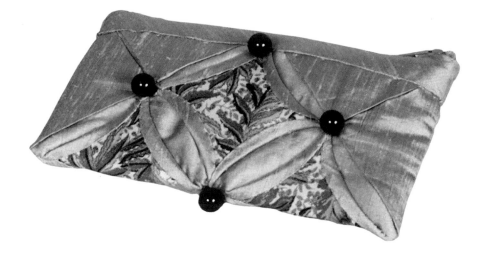

This fascinating technique was used to produce the pointed panel at the base of *Winter Days*, on page 81. Make one cardboard template, measuring 15.3 cm/6 in square, and one to the size shown on the left. For the panel, you will require 49 fabric pieces of each size. Also refer to the text on page 80. Cathedral window is stitched partly on the machine and partly by hand.

Above. Template for the centre of the cathedral window pieces (shown life size). You'll need 49 pieces for the panel at the base of Winter Days, on page 81.

Right. The evening bag and purse were made from a panel of cathedral window patchwork. A large carnelian bead was then stitched at the intersection of each piece. Photographed by Sarah Dewe.

1 Fold one large square in half.
   Machine-stitch down one side, and
   repeat for the other side, as shown.

2 Press seam open and trim corners.
   Repeat. Fold pocket across to form a
   square. Pin the open side, as shown.

In the *Winter Days* panel
(see page 81), I folded
some of the edges of the
outer squares under to form
a neat edge and left others
flat, attaching a *shisha*
to each.

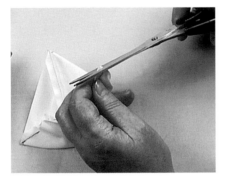

3 Machine-stitch second seam, leaving
   small gap. Press seam, trim corners.

4 The square has been turned out and
   the small gap slip-stitched by hand.

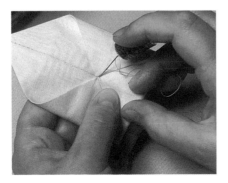

5 Bring two opposite corners towards
   the centre and anchor-stitch
   (seams uppermost); repeat. Prepare
   all large squares in this manner.

6 Join the prepared shapes along
   folded edges, oversewing them.

7 Pin coloured centres in position.
   Turn the plain coloured edges over
   the raw edges of each coloured
   square and hem-stitch neatly.

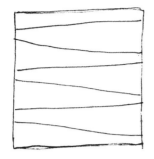

Strip Patchwork

Strip patchwork is a machine-pieced technique that is quick and easy, and can be highly effective. The small cushions shown opposite were made by this method, alternate strips being decorated with machine-embroidery (see detail below). Cut a square of cotton lawn to the eventual size of the cushion top, inclusive of the seam allowance. This foundation square will act as a kind of template.

The sketch above shows how to cut the strips.

Right and below. *This version of strip patchwork includes folded black strips, caught within the seams.*

For the strips, cut a piece of fabric slightly larger than the desired width of the cushion. Draw lines across, using a ruler to create strips that are wider at one end than the other (see the sketch on the left). Repeat this with the second colour.

Machine stitch alternate strips, joining one wide-ended strip to a narrow-ended one. When the piece is more or less square, press the seams, pushing them under the darker strip. Lay this piece over the foundation square; pin, and trim away excess fabric.

I used the same method for the background of *Summer Sprites,* on page 85 (also refer to the instructions for that piece). *Shishas* were scattered over the background, which was machine-quilted 'in the ditch' – in other words, in the seam – using silver thread. This produced an attractively sculptured surface against which the bright sunflowers stand out well.

The detail shown on the left is a variation of folded patchwork. Straight strips of black silk, cut to varying widths, were folded over, pressed; and each strip was then caught in a seam joining two of the orange strips.

Opposite. A selection of strip patchwork cushions; I normally give these cushions a plain back and finish them with a large specimen bead at each corner.

Tumbling Blocks

Tumbling blocks is a variation of English patchwork which reached the New World with the passengers of the Mayflower. Sort out your fabrics into light, medium and dark shades. Copying the sketch on the left, make a master from which to cut a paper template for each patch. Use a strong paper, but not too thick, so the templates can be used over and over again.

Lay each paper template on the wrong side of the cloth, pin and cut, keeping margins to turn under. Baste/tack the edges over the template. Organize the diamonds to form the blocks, making sure that each light, mid-toned and dark piece faces the same way. This creates the *trompe l'oeil* effect, as shown in the sketch below.

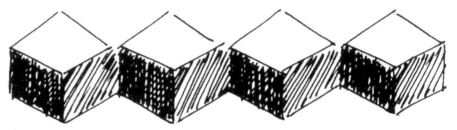

The pieces are joined by hand. Hold two diamonds with right sides together. Oversew, catching only two fabric threads on each side, working from left to right. Use a toning thread. The stitches should hardly show at all on the right side of the work.

To ensure accurate corners, assemble each block, press, then form the blocks into horizontal rows, comprising the required number of blocks. Press. Finally, join the rows among themselves and press. When the whole panel is complete and well pressed, remove the basting/tacking and the paper templates. The finished panel can now be slip-stitched in position.

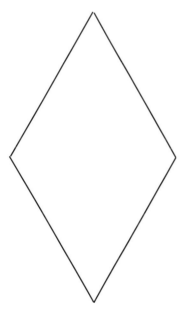

Above. The diamond template, shown life-size.

Right. A pair of cushions, each with an appliquéd tumbling-block panel. The edges of each patchwork panel were slip-stitched to the backing and machine embroidered (see crazy stitch, step 1, page 49).
Facing page: Detail from Adrift.

Quilting

The original purpose of quilting was to hold several layers of fabric together to produce a warm covering. The 'sandwich' normally comprises three layers: the top of the quilt, the batting/wadding and the backing fabric. The two lower layers should include a good margin, extending well beyond the top of the quilt. This will be trimmed off when the quilting is complete.

The sandwich should be held together by rows of tacking/basting, worked closely together, in both directions. This can be replaced by safety pins, placed at short intervals or even by ordinary pins, if the piece is small.

Whether quilting by hand or by machine, always start at the centre of the piece. This gives you some leeway to prevent puckers. When quilting around blocks, quilting (by hand or machine) can be worked a set distance from the seam or in the seam line itself, 'in the ditch'. This is the method I used for the background of *Summer Sprites*, see page 85.

Elaborate patterns can be drawn lightly, using a quilting pencil. These are supposedly erasable, but always try your pencil on a scrap of the fabric first, and check that the lines erase themselves after a while. Experienced quilters usually work by eye, drawing perhaps only the first line. When quilting a motif, always work from the centre outwards.

Hand quilting consists of rows of small regular running stitches. Elaborate quilts were usually stretched on a quilting frame, often with several women sitting along it, each responsible for a section of the quilt. Small girls learned the craft by threading needles for the workers. There is something wonderfully therapeutic about quilting. The borders and sashing of *Indian Spring Memories,* on page 69, were hand-quilted, using a light blue quilting thread to work around the 'eyes' of the tie-and-dye fabric.

Machine quilting is quicker. It can be done using straight stitching, and a quilting or an embroidery foot. A so-called 'walking foot' can be a great help, if it comes with your machine, or you find one that fits. If working with metallic thread, remember to reduce the top tension. With other threads, you may need to tighten the top tension. Every machine and thread combination is different. Once the tension is correct, insert the needle into the cloth and bring the bobbin thread up to the top. Reduce the stitch length almost to '0' and take a few tiny stitches on the spot. Return the stitch length to the desired setting, and quilt. End the stitching line in the same way as you began it. Quilt all the lines in the same direction to prevent puckering. Machine quilting can also be done using free-motion stitching and an embroidery frame. If you wish to use this method, refer to a specialist book.

Inspiration and Design

Sources of inspiration are as diverse as people themselves. I mentioned earlier on in this book that a lot of my ideas come from my childhood, from Indian visual arts, Hindu iconography, architecture from around the world, nature and poetry. This artistic vocabulary translates itself in ways that are not always recognizable to the viewer. I am personally more interested in colour play, abstract patterns, texture and constructional design than in figurative representation, but this does not mean that I disregard figurative work. One thing that I consider to be vital is to saturate one's visual memory with as many and as diverse a range of artistic influences as possible and then have a go. You may not be over-impressed with your first efforts, but your confidence will grow, and it is interesting to see how an aborted design idea sometimes re-emerges in one's consciousness and turns into a wonderful piece of work. It probably needed that period of gestation and the first unsuccessful attempt before its final flowering.

It is also very important to look at the work of other textile artists, not just embroiderers or quilters, and also to study the ways in which painters, sculptors, mosaic and other artists come to grips with the basic problem of putting their mark on a blank surface. Also work at increasing your technical knowledge of your chosen medium. Look at books, and attend classes and workshops. It is not a question of copying someone's work, but of acquiring as large a technical and inspirational repertoire as possible, while developing one's critical sense and personal style. I personally believe that the finish and the presentation of a piece of work are as important as the work itself, and I set myself high standards in this area, regardless of the time involved. I have tried to remain aloof from the controversy concerning Art versus Craft; to me the two are inextricably linked. The great Renaissance painters knew all there was to know about pigments, how they adhered to surfaces, and how they reacted to each other and their environment. Thanks to this knowledge, we can still enjoy their work today. Modern-day conservators often complain about the problems associated with the work of contemporary artists who do not possess this knowledge of their 'craft', or choose to disregard it, and whose work starts peeling off the canvas almost as the paint dries. The role of the artist and of art in society has changed greatly since the Renaissance, and in an age in which personal freedom and realization are everything, the overwhelming need to experiment may appear more important than the stability and longevity of a work of art. This is a question for the individual, whether the originator or, indeed, the buyer of the piece. You will find some guidelines on conservation in the section starting on page 122.

Textile artists are no stranger to this dilemma. Going to exhibitions, you will see all manner of experimental and innovative pieces, some of which make use of unstable materials and techniques that are unlikely to age well. I like looking at this work and am excited by it, but at the end of the day one has to evolve a personal style and make decisions about techniques and materials. Coming from a country where artisans still produce the most amazing traditional work, as well as contemporary pieces, using traditional skills, I am aware that technique and fine craftsmanship are not everything and that I want to create something which is technically competent and attractive, but – importantly – with a dimension extending beyond the merely decorative.

I am frequently asked how I get ideas and how I commit them to cloth, as it were. Whereas many people will go through a stage of elaborate drawings and workings on paper, I rarely do this, beyond very rough sketches. Like the writer agonizing in front of the blank page, I will often spend hours looking at my stock of fabrics, grouping them according to colour or texture, laying embroidery threads over them and waiting for the concept to emerge. Sometimes several days later, or as I am working on something else, glimpses begin to appear, and I eventually get a very clear picture in my mind of the proposed piece. I always carry a small notebook in my bag so that I can make a thumbnail sketch and not lose the image. I will then start straight on the cloth, at most making a couple of little samples to try out an unfamiliar technique, and work out machine tensions and colour combinations. As I'm working, the piece acquires its own momentum and sometimes develops into something substantially different from the original idea. I also frequently find myself returning to the original idea, and it becomes the starting point for a new piece of work. You will undoubtedly recognize this exploration of a design idea or source of inspiration as you leaf through the book.

Whatever your method of working, there are a few decisions that will need to be taken at the outset: the work itself, and whether this is to be figurative or abstract, the techniques to be used, the materials, the size and shape of the work, the way in which it will be hung and, often, if you are making it for yourself or as a commissioned piece, the place in which it is to hang. It is important that all the elements of a piece work harmoniously together and that the colours are balanced carefully. If you're a novice at working with colours, start with a fairly limited and sober palette and introduce colours carefully as you go along. Don't make do, using a particular shade of embroidery thread because you've got it at home, even though it's not perfectly what you had in mind; this will lead to disappointment. On the other hand, don't be afraid to experiment with colours. Combinations which seemed unpromising at first sight often turn out highly successful.

The brighter the colours, the more difficult it is to achieve a good balance. In *Summer Fever*, on page 77, for example, I was dealing with many different shades of red and contrasting them with bright greens and yellows. It was a difficult piece to balance colourwise, and I must have bought at least two lots of red silk for the borders and sashing before deciding on the correct one. Always look at your colour combination in natural and artificial light. Silk, especially, can look very different in day or nocturnal lighting, and you must make sure that your piece will look equally attractive in all lights.

When making a piece with borders and sashing, such as the *Four Seasons* pieces (pages 69, 77, 79 and 81), the width, colour and texture of the fabric for these elements can make or kill the piece. Take time to consider this before embarking on that stage. I always finish the blocks before buying the fabric for the borders. Take several of the blocks to the shop, lay them over the cloth and think hard. Should the borders and sashing be plain or patterned? Should they be darker or lighter than the blocks? Will the fabric be quilted or left flat? These decisions can radically alter the look of a piece.

When buying border or sashing fabrics, always err on the generous side, which allows you to increase the width or number of the borders, or make a mistake! Silks that are allegedly of the same colour can differ substantially from one bolt to the next.

Be strict with yourself. If you're not sure about a design decision, sleep on it, and if you don't like it, unpick or redo the offending section. The type of work you'll find in these pages is often painstakingly slow. It pays to get it right or you may regret it bitterly later on.

On page 122 you will find a section dealing with the hanging and presentation of textile pieces. Take a good look at your surroundings and what you already have on the walls. Try to hang the piece in a situation where it will be reasonably accessible, so that you can give it a good shake from time to time and avoid a build-up of dust.

If you are a novice, start out with a fairly modest piece. The joy you'll feel when it is finished will help you develop the patience and concentration to embark on a larger work. Most of all, enjoy the quiet solace which a few hours of creative sewing bring. I often come home from the office totally exhausted and pick up my embroidery to work for half an hour, to discover that I am still working, fatigue apparently forgotten, as dawn is breaking. I am sure this is excessive but I really believe that fewer people would be on Valium if there were more embroiderers among us!

Overleaf. Detail from Indian Spring Memories. *See whole piece on page 69.*

THE PROJECTS

Indian Spring Memories

SUPPLIES

- 4 m/4½ yd of white cotton lawn, 122 cm/48 in wide
- 1.5 m/1⅔ yd of fabric, 122 cm/48 in wide, for sashing and borders
- 1.8 m/2 yd, of 135 gm/4 oz wadding/batting
- 30cm/10in of firm calico, 122 cm/48 in wide, for a sleeve
- A large selection of fabrics – silks, cottons, linen, velvets, lace etc
- A variety of hand and machine embroidery threads (rayon, stranded cotton, floss silk, embroidery ribbon, metallic thread, wool etc)
- Braid and ribbon
- *Shishas*, buttons, embroidery and specimen beads, semi-precious stones, scarabs and other found objects

Opposite. The finished hanging measures 138 x 112 cm/ 54 x 44 in. All the embroidery and most of the quilting on this piece were stitched entirely by hand. Photographed by Sarah Dewe.

This hanging forms part of a series of four, which represent the seasons. It is made of crazy patchwork, embellished with Indian and western hand embroidery, used in a non-traditional manner. The fabrics are mostly Indian silks (a few recycled from antique saris), but also include indigo-dyed cotton damask from Guinea, velvets, hand-dyed cottons and antique lace. The embellishments include Indian *shishas*, braids and ribbons, Suffolk puffs, glass beads, semi-precious stones, buttons, scarabs and other found objects. Imprinted on my mind are the colours and memories of spring in Northern India – a season which is all too short, yet magical – the deep blue of the sky at night, the pink hues of dawn rising over the river, the vivid green of the young plants and the intoxicating scent of mango blossoms. There is a tremendous feeling of pulsating life. March soon comes to an end, however, and with the arrival of April, the temperature rises with each passing day, bringing in the implacable Indian summer heat.

1   The background of the hanging is made of crazy patchwork. Originally, crazy patchwork was devised as a means of using the tiniest scraps of fabric, the edges of which were often left raw and then covered with a row of herringbone stitches. It was the recycling end of patchwork *par excellence*. I love the effect created by the crazy pattern, but I want to harness its potentials: the shapes, the colours, the weights of the different fabrics and the positioning of each piece is carefully thought out. I use a method which is half-way between conventional crazy patchwork and appliqué (see page 55).

2   Assemble all your selected fabrics and begin to look for pleasant colour combinations as well as attractive or unusual contrasts of texture and weight. This is also the time when you'll be able to see if you need to increase your palette by buying a few more colours or dying silk to suit.

3   Cut nine 30 cm/12 in squares of cotton lawn. These will form the foundation for the nine crazy patchwork blocks.

4   Referring to page 55 for the step-by-step method, pin the first piece in the corner of the first block. Press the edge of the second piece, lay it over the raw edge of the first, and pin. Continue in this fashion until the entire block is covered with pinned pieces. Look at this block critically and check that the arrangement is pleasing. You may wish to change one or more of the pieces, or alter their shape. Don't start sewing at this stage, but prepare the second block instead, continuing until all nine are completed.

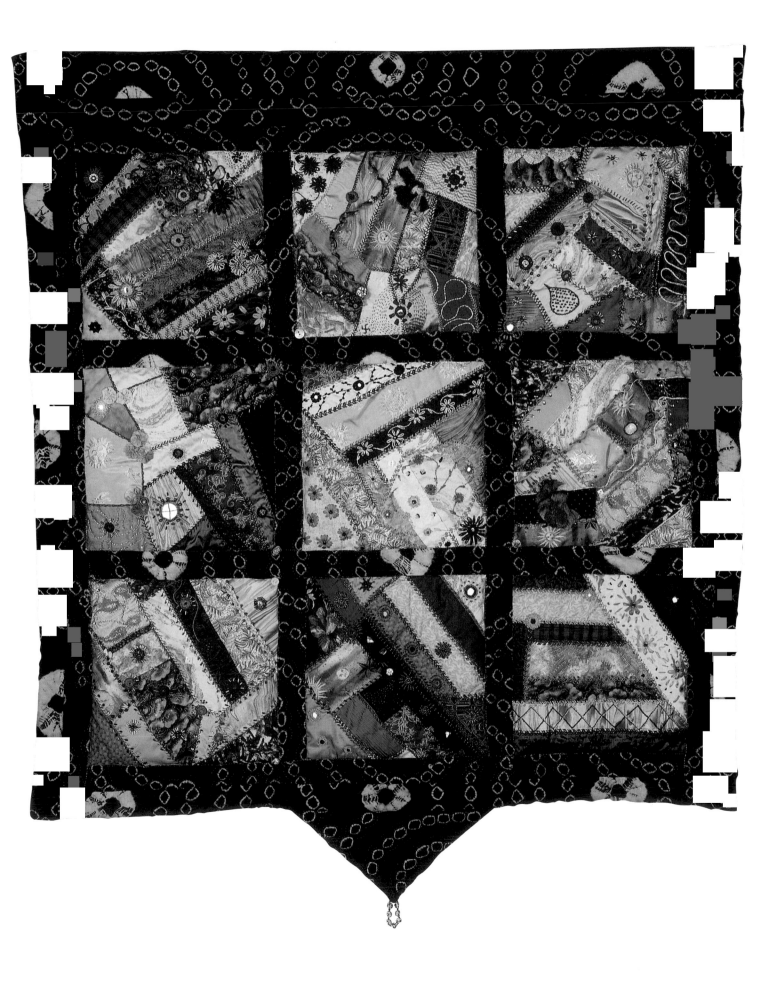

All measurements given from now on include 6 mm/¼ in seam allowances, unless otherwise specified.

Below (detail) and opposite. The panels on the cushions were worked in exactly the same way as the blocks in the hanging. The panels were then tacked/basted over a plain cushion front and the raw edges covered with braid.

5 As you gradually cover the blocks, keep looking at them to see whether the contrasts between light and dark, matt and shiny fabrics, weights and textures are balanced, both within each block and among the blocks. Replace individual pieces if necessary. This is why I don't start sewing until all the blocks are made up.

6 Arrange your nine blocks on the floor in the order in which they will appear in the finished piece. Number them at the back, marking the top of each block.

7 Slip-stitch the pinned pieces. This can be done quickly, as the edges of each piece will be reinforced by feather stitch and beading. Finish off all nine blocks. Press.

8 Your 'canvas' is now ready and you can embark on the embroidery. I covered all the edges of the crazy patchwork with feather or herringbone stitches. Create focal points in each block by working a 'clump' of embroidery – see the detail opposite of the single shisha surrounded by beading or the group of pink flowers worked in silk ribbon. The couched embroidery, worked with blue wool and a variety of yarns, is also very effective (see the top left-hand corner of the detail on page 66).

The texture is built up gradually by the addition of *shishas*, sequins and beads. After working the focal point of the block, attach the *shishas*. Lay them on the piece first and work out where you want them to go. Using a quilting pencil, circle around them, but keep your lines very light. In theory, lines drawn with a quilting pencil should erase themselves pretty quickly. Do not trust the theory as it depends very much on the fabric! Very simple techniques, such as a running stitch worked around the pattern of a printed fabric, with either a toning or contrasting thread, can be highly effective. *Kantha* quilting can produce a variety effects, depending on whether you use tiny or longer stitches, or work over a soft fabric, such as real silk satin, or over a crisp linen. A range of speckling and filling stitches can break up plain areas or tone down a strongly coloured piece (see page 35). Because you are already working on a double layer of fabric, you are creating texture which, along with the *shishas* and the glossy silks, will trap light and produce a rich, intricate surface. You can appliqué scraps of antique lace, Suffolk puffs, manipulated fabrics and ribbon. Above all, use your imagination and own taste to decorate each block, making it as elaborate or keeping it as simple as you wish.

9 Keep the beading for the last, as embroidery threads can become caught in it. I covered all the edges of the crazy pattern with embroidery beads, carefully choosing their colours to tone up with the feather-stitch embroidery. You can

contrast sparkling and matt glass beads. I use a doubled matching sewing thread to attach the beads, passing it through each bead twice. Every few beads, I work a few stitches at the back of the work and start again. This means that should the thread break, two or three beads may drop off but the whole row will not unravel. Stitch buttons, scarabs and specimen beads firmly into place. Position the blocks in the right order on the floor and check that the embellishments are balanced and form a harmonious whole. Press.

If you are combining embroidery and beading in one block, always try to work the embroidery first. In this way, the thread won't become entangled with the beads.

10 The sketch on the opposite page shows how the hanging was assembled. Cut six pieces, each 30 x 6 cm/11⅞ x 2⅜ in, from the fabric selected for the sashing. These are the short pieces between the blocks, coloured green and marked *a* on the sketch. These and all further measurements include a 6 mm/¼ in seam allowance. Assemble the first three blocks to form the top row of the hanging. Repeat for the other blocks. Press flat.

11 Measure the length of the top row. Cut four strips of fabric – horizontal strips *b* – to that length and 30 x 6 cm/11⅞ x 2⅜ in wide. Assemble as shown. Press.

12 Measure the sides of the panel and cut two strips – marked *c* – to that length and 6 cm/2⅜ in wide, shown in pale blue on the sketch. Assemble as shown. Press.

13 The top of the hanging is now finished. Measure it, and cut a piece of cotton lawn and also one of wadding/batting 15 cm/6 in larger all round than the hanging. Lay the lawn right side down on the floor, then the wadding, then the quilt, right side uppermost. Starting from the centre of the piece, baste/tack all layers together at 7½ cm/3 in intervals, first across the width, then across the height. Trim the batting/wadding and lawn layer so that it extends 10 cm/4 in beyond the top of the hanging.

14 Measure the top, including the batting/wadding , and cut 2 strips to that length and 24 cm/9½ in wide. Press in half along the length. These will form the top and bottom outer borders – *d* in the sketch. Pin the raw edge of *d* strips to the edge of each *b* strip. Machine-stitch. Press seam. Turn edge under and hand-hem.

15 Measure the raw sides of the hanging. Cut two strips to that length and 24 cm/9½ in wide. Proceed as in step 14 to form borders marked *e*.

16 To make the hanging sleeve, marked *f*, measure the top of the hanging. Cut one piece of the border fabric to that length, adding seam allowances, and 25 cm/10 in in width. Cut a similar piece of firm calico to line the sleeve. Join the two pieces along their short sides. Turn out and press. Fold and machine-stitch to form a tube. Zigzag the raw edges. Slip-stitch this sleeve to the back of the top border.

17 The pointed panel – *g* – is made up of a triangle of main fabric, 43 cm/17 in wide and 19 cm/7½ in deep. Line this with batting/wadding and lawn, as for the blocks.

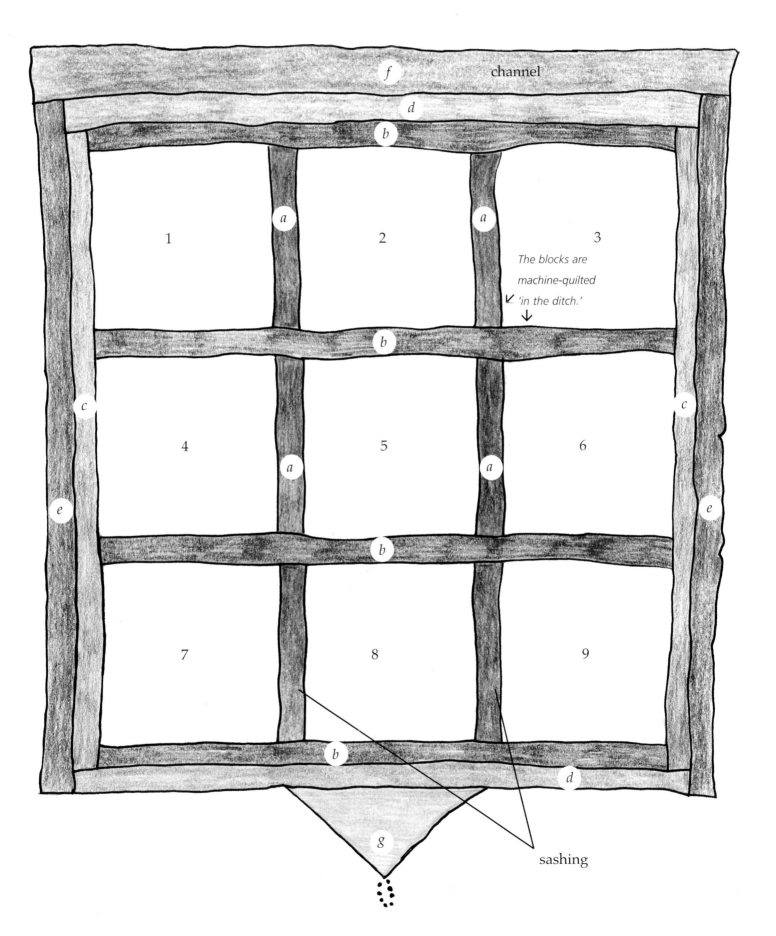

channel

The blocks are
machine-quilted
'in the ditch.'

sashing

Opposite page. Blue Window measures 175 x 39 cm/ 69 x 15½ in. Reproduced by kind permission of Simon and Barbara Grandage.

Below. It is a quilting tradition to fix a personalized label at the back of the finished quilt. I usually embroider the edge to tone up with the piece, recording the title of the piece, my name, and the date of completion.

18 The hanging is now ready for quilting. Start in the centre of the hanging. I machine-quilted 'in the ditch' around the blocks and along the borders, using a silver metallic thread. I then hand-quilted sashing strips *a*, *b* and *c*, using a pale blue thread around the 'eyes' of the tie-dyed fabric. Repeat for panel *g*.

19 You can now finish off the pointed panel *g*. Trim away the excess batting/wadding. Cut a triangle of toning blue silk to the same size. Place this on panel *g*, with right sides together. Machine-stitch down both sides to the point, adding a string of beads or a large tassel so that it is caught in the seam. Turn right side out. Press and slip-stitch behind the bottom border *d*.

20 Measure the hanging, excluding the hanging sleeve, and cut a lawn backing. Turn down a 6 mm/¼ in all round and press. Pin the backing to the hanging and slip-stitch. Embroider your personalized label and slip-stitch it in position. All you need is a stout pole, and the piece is ready to be hung.

Blue Window

This piece was commissioned to fit a particular space in the home of a client who had seen *Along the Golden Path,* page 83, and liked it, especially the crazy patchwork background. She wanted a longer piece, however, and specified a colour scheme including turquoise blue and dashes of pink.

I felt that such a long piece – 175 x 39 cm/69 x 15½ in – required a strongly defined top, and gradually the image of a tall leaded window began to emerge. The client has a passion for Venice, and this is suggested by the shaped window 'frame'. I drew a paper template of the top, and lined a piece of black silk with a fusible fabric/Bondaweb and cotton lawn, see page 52. The shape was then cut out, using the paper template. The curved edge was finished off with a machine-satin stitch on a medium width setting, using an oxidized machine embroidery thread. Lines of straight machine stitching, using a variegated metallic embroidery thread, were worked over the silk and overlaid with hand embroidery (daisy stitch flowers), *shishas* and beads.

I then cut the foundation lawn to the whole size of the hanging. Indian and Thai silks were used for the crazy patchwork. I included some small pieces of hand-printed velvet donated by a textile artist friend, Anna Steiner. These shimmered with jewel-like colours that were perfect for the stained-glass window. The crazy patchwork was done in the usual way (see page 55) but instead of outlining the patches with hand or machine feather stitch, I selected the satin machine stitch again, set at its widest setting, and used a dark silver metallic thread. Some of the patches were first outlined with narrow black ribbon, and the satin stitch was worked over this (see detail on page 54). I included a lot of *shishas*, each daintily outlined with glass beads, and flowers hand-embroidered in rayon thread and in embroidery ribbon. I then lined the whole piece with domett before attaching a few Venetian glass specimen beads. Using fabric adhesive, I added two old Indian coins for luck, plus fragments of abalone shell and the eye of a peacock feather.

The top section was attached to the front of the hanging. The raw outer edges were finished with narrow strips of black silk. These were turned under and the edges machine-quilted 'in the ditch', see page 62. The base was weighted with small leads. A batten and rings were attached at the top to hang the piece (see page 124), which was lined with an opaque fabric.

Summer Fever

This piece is the second in the *Four Seasons* series. The vibrant colours are reminiscent of the sub-tropical vegetation of South India. The construction of the hanging was kept plain to give maximum impact to the colour scheme and to the intricately embroidered and beaded surface.

SUPPLIES

- 4 m/4½ yd of white cotton lawn, 122 cm/48 in wide
- 115 cm/45 in of plain fabric, 122 cm/48 in wide, for borders
- 8.2 m/9 yd of satin ribbon, 5 cm/2 in wide, for sashing
- 1.8 m/2 yd of 135 gm/4 oz batting/wadding
- Selection of assorted fabrics and threads, mother-of-pearl buttons, semi-precious stone, glass and specimen beads, and other found objects

Opposite page and below (detail). Summer Fever *is part of the* Four Seasons *series. The finished piece measures 109 x 113 cm/43 x 44½ in.*

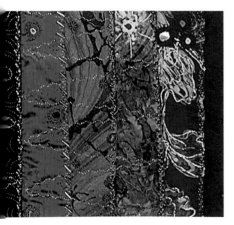

1   Turn to *Indian Spring Memories*, page 68, and follow steps 1–6 inclusive. For *Summer Fever*, I have used the machine's fagotting stitch to outline the edges of the crazy patchwork. This means that in step 7 you need not slip-stitch the edges of the pieces, but can proceed with the machine embroidery, stitching straight over the pins and using a variety of gold threads.

2   Proceed as in steps 8 and 9 of *Indian Spring*. Machine embroidery was mixed with the hand work and beading.

3   Cut a piece of cotton lawn, 1 m/39½ in square, and lay it flat. Pin the first three top blocks over this foundation, leaving 4 cm/1½ in gaps between them (guidelines can be drawn on the foundation first, if you prefer). Proceed for the second row, leaving the same gap between this and the first row. Position the bottom row, and baste/tack the blocks in position, making sure that the outer edges of the piece are square. Small adjustments can be made at this stage (due to machine tension and the weight of the embroidery, some of the blocks may end up smaller than their neighbours).

4   Cut six pieces of ribbon, each 32 cm/13 in long. These will provide the short pieces of sashing between the blocks. Pin and slip-stitch them into position. Measure the long gaps between the rows of blocks and cut strips of ribbon to the appropriate length. Pin and stitch them as before. Repeat for the outer edges of the hanging, starting with the two sides, and then the top and bottom of the piece. Press.

5   The borders are made of strips, each 12½ cm/5 in wide, cut out of the plain silk and reinforced with fine cotton lawn. They are attached to the edges of the hanging. The piece is now ready to be placed over the batting/wadding and the foundation lawn. Baste/tack in readiness for hand-quilting close to the edge of the sashing, along the borders and following the outlines of the crazy patchwork.

6   To finish the borders, fold over and pin the plain strip, covering its batting /wadding and lawn lining, first along the two sides of the hanging then along the

bottom. Slip-stitch the raw edges to the back. The hanging sleeve is produced by machine-stitching one side of a strip of strong calico to the free edge of the top border and fixing its other edge to the back of the hanging. Slip-stitch the final backing, covering the raw edges.

Mellow Fruitfulness

SUPPLIES

- 4 m/4½ yd of white cotton lawn, 122 cm/48 in wide
- 1.5 m/1⅔ yd of fabric, 122 cm/48 in wide, for borders and sashing
- 1.8 m/2 yd of 135 gm/4 oz wadding/batting
- A selection of assorted fabrics and threads, mother-of-pearl buttons, semi-precious stones, beads and other found objects

Opposite page and below (detail). The hanging measures 143 x 94 cm/ 56½ x 37 in. Photographed by Curtis Lane & Co.

The brilliant colours of this wallhanging attempt to convey the glory of autumn. It also forms part of the *Four Seasons* series, the first of which is shown on page 69. The beautiful burnt-orange silk and metallic fabric used for the borders and sashing of *Mellow Fruitfulness* was quite stiff and, once quilted, it caught the light beautifully. I covered large areas of the hanging with free-hand machine-embroidery, using a Güttermann metallic thread, which comes in an attractive and 'autumnal' copper colour. I then worked the hand embroidery and the beading over it, building up the textures. I used various densities of *kantha* quilting (see page 36), often to produce simple concentric patterns, as shown below left.

Most of the fabrics used are silks, some of which are hand-dyed, but the work also includes cottons, velvets and linen. I used a wide variety of embellishments, ranging from lace, braid, precious Venetian hand-made glass buttons and mother-of-pearl buttons to the many *shishas,* which often form the centre of large stylized flowers, decorated with embroidery and beading. Semi-precious stone beads – carnelian, amber and tiger's eye – complement the rich colour scheme. The pointed panel at the base of the hanging is also heavily embroidered, with couched work, which in turn is encrusted with *shishas* and beads.

The blocks are all exactly the same size and are worked in a similar way to those of *Indian Spring Memories*, on page 68. I used machine fagotting stitch and various metallic embroidery threads to define the edges of the patchwork. The piece is quilted 'in the ditch' around the blocks.

The construction of the hanging is slightly simpler than that of *Indian Spring Memories*, but small squares of brown silk were inserted into the sashing. Looking at the sketch on page 73, the vertical strips – *a* – are the same in the autumn hanging. It is when you come to *b* that there is a difference. Instead of cutting long strips, cut small strips, as for *a*, and the required number of squares to the width of the strip. Machine-stitch short strips and squares to form a continuous row, and pin this to the bottom of the assembled first three blocks, making sure that the squares butt accurately with the edges of the vertical strips. You may need to ease the work gradually across the width of the block to make sure the squares fit neatly. Simple geometric patterns were hand-quilted on the top and bottom borders.

Winter Days

SUPPLIES

- 4 m/4½ yd of white cotton lawn, 122 cm/48 in wide
- 1.5 m/1⅔ yd of fabric, 122 cm/48 in wide, for borders and sashing
- 1.8 m/2 yd of 135 gm/4 oz wadding/batting
- Selection of fabrics for the crazy and cathedral window patchworks
- Threads; mother-of-pearl buttons, semi-precious stone beads, feathers and other found objects

Double ruching

Cut a piece of fabric at least five times larger than the desired result (perhaps more if the fabric is very flimsy). Thread the machine with matching thread, lowering the tension so that the stitching is very loose, and stitch parallel lines, 6 mm/¼ in apart. Do not secure the ends, but allow the lengths of thread to hang freely, at the beginning and end. Repeat in the other direction. Pull gathers, first on one side, and then on the other, scrunching up the cloth tightly. Secure the thread ends.

This wallhanging completes the cycle of the *Four Seasons*. Here, the browns, greys and dull greens are contrasted with creams, white and silver, with touches of sky-blue and pale pink. Note the tiny dabs of bright red in each block. Some years ago, I was fortunate to work on a wonderful nature book. The author was a naturalist, as well as an accomplished artist. She was one of those rare people who had managed to preserve something of the child's sense of wonder. She never saw winter as drab and devoid of colour. She pointed to the crop of rose hips and hawthorn berries shining in the hedges, the flash of red on a robin's throat and the rich brown of oak leaves outlined with rime. Suddenly, the landscape turned into the kingdom of the Snow Queen. I never forgot what she made me see and wanted to recall something of her vision in this piece.

The blocks are heavily embroidered and beaded, using much *kantha* quilting, worked at varying densities and stitch lengths. The deep panel at the base of the hanging is made up of 49 cathedral window patchwork pieces (see page 56 for basic method and size of pieces), in carefully graded colours. I tea-dyed some of the silks to get the delicate shading I wanted. The aim was to create a contrast between the shiny metallic silks, used for some of the 'window frames', with a dull indigo, block-printed Japanese hemp fabric, which was entirely matt and which I used for some of the small squares at the centre of the windows. Here again, a couple of red pieces bring the colour scheme to life.

In the crazy patchwork, besides the usual silks, I used some winter-weight woollen fabrics, velvets, grey lace and other unexpected materials. I have also used double ruching (see note opposite) and included wooden beads and feathers among the *shishas*.

A line of hand-quilting was worked 6 mm/¼ in away from the edges of the blocks. The narrow sashing is hand-quilted down the middle, and a simple pattern worked over the top and bottom borders. The top of the hanging is folded upon itself to form a channel for the pole. The *shishas* on the top border were applied at the same time as the quilting, making sure that the stitches went right through the sandwich, a little like buttons on upholstery.

Winter Days measures
144 x 88 cm/57 x 35 in.
Photographed by Curtis
Lane & Co.

Along the Golden Path

This piece was the precursor to *Blue Window*, on page 75. The method used is crazy patchwork, but many of the patches have been cut almost in horizontal strip form. The embroidery and decoration are more restrained than in the large hangings which form part of the *Four-Seasons* series, yet the piece has a rich and warm feel, created by the judicious use of colours and patterns.

I first cut an oblong of cotton lawn, 155 x 44 cm/61 x 17½ in, for the foundation and ran a line of tacking/basting to mark the edges of the finished piece, 150 x 39 cm/59 x 15½ in. I chose the fabrics and organized them in pleasing 'families' (see crazy patchwork method, page 55). For once, I used a few man-made fabrics, chosen for the beauty of their textures and patterns, among the usual silks and cottons. Some of the strips are attached to the foundation cloth on one side only, while the raw edge of each overlaps the next patch and becomes a feature. *Shisha* work and simple machine and hand embroidery were worked over each patch, running from left to right, encouraging the eye to travel across and down, as along a well-ordered path. I also incorporated antique and modern lace. Modern cotton lace would have looked too stark, so I dyed it in strong tea to make it blend with the colour scheme. The machine embroidery is mostly tone on tone, giving the fabric texture rather than decoration.

The piece of domett is cut to the exact finished size of the piece and tacked/basted to the back of the work. Trim excess foundation cloth if necessary, and fold the edges of the work over the domett, slip-stitching them to the back. Add a few specimen beads, making sure that the stitching goes right through the layers. As this piece is not quilted, it is quite a good idea to attach the layers by running lines of slip stitches along the edges of some of the patches, making sure the stitches do not show on the top. Line the back with cotton lawn.

The top of the piece was finished with the flat batten method (see page 124). Instead of the rings which I normally attach under the batten, I made a cord by braiding oddments of cotton perlé and other embroidery threads in toning colours. Attach your personalized label.

SUPPLIES

- 2 oblongs, 155 x 44 cm/ 61 x 17½ in, one of cotton lawn and one of domett
- A selection of silk, cotton and synthetic fabrics
- DMC stranded cotton and rayon hand embroidery threads; Güttermann copper, gold and green metallic machine embroidery threads
- Lace, glass and specimen beads

Opposite page. A detail of Along the Golden Path.
Far right. The finished piece, 150 x 39 cm/ 59 x 15½ in.

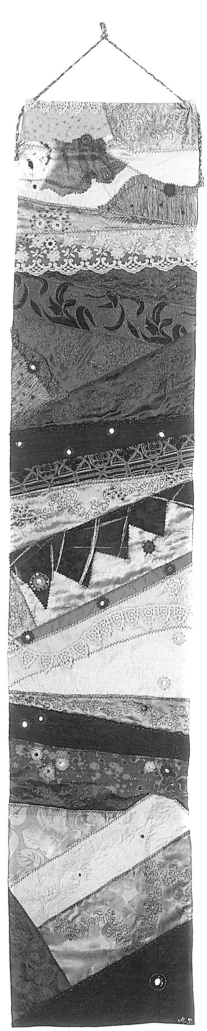

Summer Sprites

A painting by an American artist – whose name I failed to note – was the catalyst for this piece. The picture showed a bouquet of sunflowers standing in a blue jar and painted in a highly realistic, almost photographic style. Propped against the jar was a home-made get-well card with a naïve picture of another bunch of sunflowers, as if drawn by an eight-year-old. I was enchanted with this child-like representation of a flower I have always loved. I remembered the huge top-heavy specimens, so common in Indian villages, and also the marvellous sight of fields in southern Spain with their thousands of little faces turned towards the sun. A friend's gift of a piece of yellow silk, purchased in Thailand, reminded me of the painting, and a picture of naïve sunflowers, standing proud over a heavily sculpted panel, made of quilted strip patchwork, began to form in my mind.

SUPPLIES

- Silks – 1 m/40 in of dark brown; 50 cm/20 in each of bronze and white; 66 x 46 cm/26 x 18 in of yellow, and 30 cm/12 in of green, for leaves and stems
- 69 cm/27 in of fusible fabric/Bondaweb
- 2.4 m/2²/3 yd of white lawn, for foundation and backing etc
- 1 m/40 in of calico or other opaque fabric, for final backing
- 1 m/40 in of light-weight batting/wadding
- *Shishas*
- DMC rayon embroidery threads, and Madeira metallic machine embroidery threads
- Matching sewing threads
- 61 cm/24 in length of small curtain leads, to weight the hanging

1 For the strip patchwork background, cut six strips of brown silk, each 97 cm/ 38¹/₂ in in length and approximately 6 cm/2¹/₄ in at one end and 4 cm/1¹/₂ in at the other. Don't try to make every strip exactly the same width – the slightly random effect adds interest to the technique (see page 58). Machine-stitch the strips, joining a narrow end to a large one and alternating the colours (refer to photograph of hanging). Press, pushing the seams under the darker strips to conceal them.

2 You now have to trim the patchwork to a rectangle: take the shortest measurement each way, and cut an oblong of cotton lawn to that size. Lay the patchwork over this cotton foundation, and pin it in position. Machine-stitch around the edge. Trim away the excess fabric, and run a zigzag stitch all around the piece to prevent fraying. The resulting piece of fabric should measure approximately 97 x 59 cm/23¹/₂ x 38 in.

3 For the appliqued sunflowers, first back the piece of yellow silk with cotton lawn, using fusible webbing (Bondaweb), as explained on page 52, in readiness for cutting out the flower petals.

4 Trace the petal, flower centre and leaf pattern shown on page 87, and make templates out of thin card.

5 Using the petal template, trace 56 petals on the cotton side of the prepared piece of yellow silk. Machine stay-stitch over the pencil line around each petal, using a toning sewing thread. Cut out the petals immediately outside the line of stitching.

Opposite. Summer Sprites
99 x 55 cm/39 x 22 in.

Above. Detail of the flower and its centre. Below. Arranging the petals to form the flower.

6 Divide the petals into three groups of 16 and one group of 8. Using a machine embroidery thread of your choice, work a machine satin stitch (see page 50) over the long sides of the first 16 petals, stopping 1cm/¹/₂ in short of the base of the petal. This will avoid unsightly bulk under the centre of the flower. When working a satin stitch around a pointed shape, such as a petal or a leaf, start stitching as close to the point as possible, with the stitch width at its narrowest setting. Increase the width of the stitch gradually. Start near the base of the second side and work up towards the point, decreasing the width of the stitch as you reach the top. This will ensure a neat point. This may require a little practice, especially when you are using metallic embroidery threads.

7 Take 8 petals out of the 16 you have just worked, and add either a single line of satin stitch or lines of straight stitching along the centre of each petal. It is nice to vary the pattern slightly between the different flowers. If you look at the picture of the hanging on page 85, you will see that I have also used different threads to embroider the petals of each flower. Repeat for the other two flowers and the half flower, and press.

8 To form a flower, first place the flower centre template down on the table. Arrange the eight plain petals over its edge, as shown on the sketch opposite. In this way, the raw edges of the petals will eventually be hidden by the flower centre. Lay the remaining eight petals over the gaps, so that they overlap with the first layer. Hand-stitch the petals together at the base. Repeat for the other two flowers and the half flower. Arrange the flowers over the background panel and tack/baste them in place.

9 Take a piece of brown silk, large enough to contain four flower centres, and back it with fusible fabric/Bondaweb, exactly as for the petals. Mark and cut out the shapes. Stay-stitch each shape and work a grid of small squares, using a metallic brown/gold embroidery thread, over the circles. Press, and then pin a circle to the centre of each flower. Work a row of wide satin stitch to cover the edges of the flower centres.

10 For the stems and leaves, first cut a strip of green silk, 4 cm/1¹/₂ in wide and approximately 70 cm/27¹/₂ in long. Cut a slightly narrower strip of domett. Place the domett over the silk strip, and roll the two together to make a thin 'sausage'; this will form the tall flower stem. Turn the raw edge of the silk under, pin and slip-stitch, making sure that the roll is the same diameter all along. Prepare the shorter stem in the same way; this is only 25 cm/10 in long. These measurements

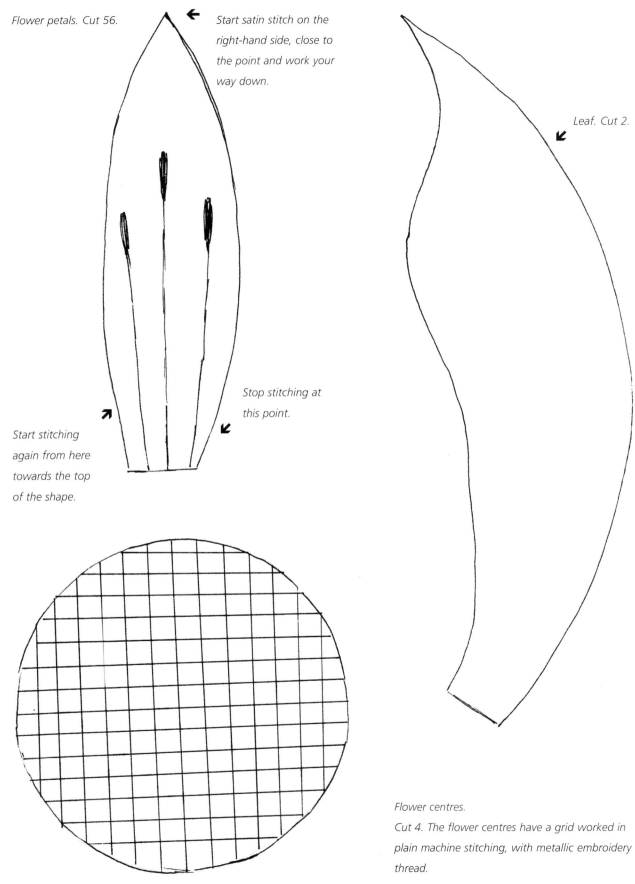

Flower petals. Cut 56.

Start satin stitch on the right-hand side, close to the point and work your way down.

Stop stitching at this point.

Start stitching again from here towards the top of the shape.

Leaf. Cut 2.

Flower centres.
Cut 4. The flower centres have a grid worked in plain machine stitching, with metallic embroidery thread.

are, of course, approximate as their length will depend on the way you position the flowers against the background. Press lightly.

11 Prepare two leaf shapes in the same way as the petals, making sure that they are mirror shapes of each other. Work a satin stitch at the edge to form a curving shape along the centre.

12 Push the ends of the stems under the petals of their respective flowers. Each stem should fit in the centre of a background stripe (see detail of hanging on the opposite page).

13 Lay the piece on the table and position the *shishas* as desired. Trace around them lightly, using a quilting pencil, and embroider them, using rayon hand-embroidery threads in your chosen colours. Press.

14 To quilt the background, first cut an oblong of batting/wadding and one of cotton lawn, both at least 8 cm/3 in larger all around than the background panel. Place the lawn face down on the table; cover it with the batting/wadding, and finally centre the background panel over the top. Starting from the centre of the piece, place pins or run lines of gathering thread, no more than 5 cm/2 in apart, along each seam of the strip patchwork, coming as close as possible to the centre of each flower. Starting from the centre of the piece and using a metallic thread, machine quilt 'in the ditch' along each seam of the patchwork, reaching under the flower petals. (See basic quilting method on page 62.)

15 Trim away the excess batting/wadding and the lawn. Measure the long sides of the hanging. From the remaining brown silk, cut two strips to that length and each 8 cm/3¼ in wide. Machine-stitch one to each edge. Turn under, and press seam and hem. Repeat for the two short sides.

16 To make loops, cut four strips of silk, each 18 cm/7 in wide, to the desired length (dictated by the diameter of the pole). If the silk is lightweight, line it with cotton lawn, possibly using fusible fabric (Bondaweb) to give body to the loops. Fold each strip in half and machine-stitch. Turn each strip right side out, placing the seam at the centre of the (inner) side. Press, and attach to the back of the hanging.

17 Give the flower petals a final press. Make a tiny stitch at the tip of each upper petal, using the same thread as the machine satin stitch, to attach it to the

background and prevent it from flapping, while allowing it to retain some measure of movement. Do the same at the tips of the leaves.

18 Slip-stitch the length of lead weights 6.5 cm/$2^{1/2}$ in away from the bottom of the hanging and from the sides. Finally, cut an oblong of cotton calico or other fairly heavy fabric for the final backing. Turn the edges under and slip-stitch in position, allowing some 5 cm/2 in of the silk border to show. This will give weight to the piece and make it hang well. Prepare the personalized label and slip-stitch it in position.

Detail of the leaf and stem.

Dawn Blooms

SUPPLIES

- 1.3 m/1½ yd of strong, closely woven silk
- 1.3 m/1½ yd of fine cotton lawn
- 30 cm/12 in each of white silk fabric for petals; of silver cloth for bracts, and of white organdi for the centres of the flowers
- 1 m/40 in of lightweight polyester batting/wadding, and a small amount of quilting wool
- 1 m/40 in of cotton calico or other fabric for backing
- 19 *shishas*
- 14 small mother-of-pearl buttons
- Small clear glass beads and pearls
- DMC rayon hand embroidery rayon thread and machine embroidery thread; Madeira machine embroidery thread in pale silver
- 60 cm/22 in length of small curtain leads, to weight the hanging

This piece is similar in concept to *Summer Sprites,* on page 85, but its background is a solid piece of silk rather than strip patchwork.

1 Cut an oblong of silk, measuring 100 x 56 cm/39½ x 22 in. Line this with cotton lawn and neaten the edges as usual. Draw the eight quilting lines free-hand over the silk, using a quilting pencil. Keep the lines as fine and as faint as possible; quilting pencil lines are supposed to erase themselves after a time, but do not believe it! Proceed to make the flowers.

2 I used three shades of white, cream and the palest of pink for the flowers. The bracts are made of an Indian raw silk, woven with silver lurex, which has a lot of body. Trace the petal and bract shapes shown opposite, and make templates out of thin card. Then refer to steps 3 to 8 on pages 84 and 86. Work a satin stitch around the petals and the bracts. The pattern over the petals is formed by lengths of straight machine stitching. When arranging the petals, note that in this case a deep pleat was made at the base of each petal to reduce its width under the heart of the flower (see the photograph of the finished piece, on page 93). Arrange the bracts in a circle; make a pleat at the base of each of the four petals, and lay these over the bracts, leaving a small circular gap in the middle of the flower. This will be covered by the heart. Slip-stitch bracts and petals together.

3 To make the flower centres, fold the length of organdi across its width, and cover three circles, each approximately 11½ cm/4½ in in diameter, with free-hand machine embroidery, using crazy stitch worked in silver thread (see page 49). Cut out the embroidered circles and run a row of gathers, close to the edge around each. Pull the thread so that the raw edge turns under by 12 mm/½ in to form a small puff, approximately 9 cm/3½ in in diameter. Insert a small amount of quilting wool and work a loose chevron stitch over the raw edge of the fabric to prevent fraying and hold the wool inside the puff. Press lightly.

4 Position the flowers over the background, but do not attach them to it at this stage. Arrange the *shishas* and the mother-of-pearl buttons, always between two quilting lines, and mark their positions. Remove the flowers, and embroider the *shishas*. Work the three star motifs around each *shisha* as shown below, stopping short of the quilting lines.

5 Refer to steps 14 and 15 on page 88, and quilt along the pencilled lines, using silver thread. Finish off the background, as explained.

Enlarge the two shapes shown below by 200 per cent on a photocopier and prepare templates out of thin card.

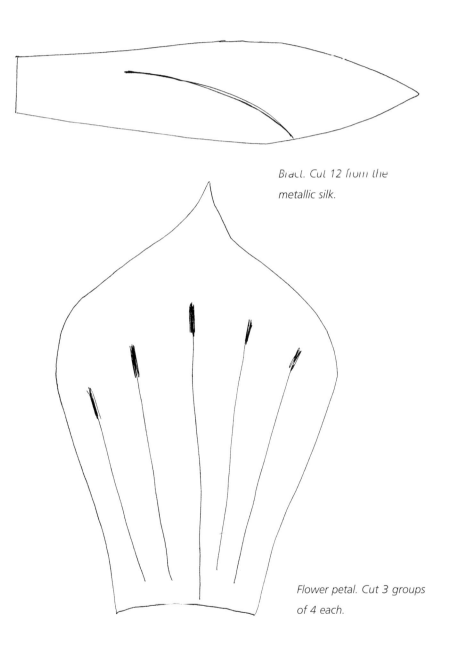

Bract. Cut 12 from the metallic silk.

Flower petal. Cut 3 groups of 4 each.

6   Attach each flower to the background by stitching around the base of the petals/bracts, taking the stitches right through the quilted background. Slip-stitch the flower centres in position. Give the petals a final touching-up with the iron. A tiny stitch, and small glass beads or pearls were used to attach the loose ends of the bracts and petals. Do not stitch every bead in the same position – they are meant to look like dew drops!

7   The sleeve for the pole was made from a strip of silk, 18 cm/7 in wide, prepared as explained in step 16 on page 72. Attach the sleeve to the back of the hanging. Stitch the line of leads at the base of the back, and attach the backing and the personalized label as explained in step 18, page 89.

8   The pole was cut to the exact width of the hanging and finished off with attractive ceramic finials from Rajasthan. Normally used as knobs on cabinet drawers, these provide a smart finish for the wallhanging.

Night Blooms (see overleaf), 105 x 60 cm/41^1/$_2$ x 23^1/$_2$ in, is another piece that includes appliquéd flowers, the centre of each flower being worked in double ruching (see marginal note on page 80). The entire background was worked with a grid, executed free-hand in large running stitches, using silver thread, so that it looks like a piece of loose netting. *Shisha* work and free-motion machine embroidery, enhanced with hand stitchery and tiny embroidery beads, provide further texture. The hand embroidery colours echo the rich border and the hearts of the flowers.

Next page. Night Blooms.

Opposite page. Dawn Blooms, *38^1/$_2$ x 21^1/$_4$ in/ 97^1/$_2$ x 54 cm.*

Detail from the hanging, showing the machine-embroidered silver star, surrounding a shisha.

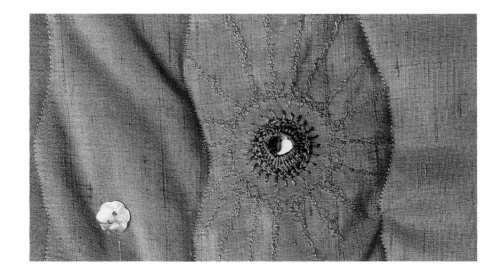

Seminole Abstractions

SUPPLIES

- 1 m/40 in each of white moiré and of black slub silk
- 1.7 m/2 yd of red shot silk
- Two 90 x 62 cm/35½ x 24½ in oblongs of cotton lawn, and one each of domett and cream calico
- DMC rayon hand embroidery threads in pale grey and red; Madeira machine embroidery threads in black, white, and metallic silver
- Embroidery beads, larger silver beads, and matching sequins
- 20 *shishas*

The base for this piece is seminole patchwork, a technique developed by the Seminole Indians in the United States when they were first introduced to the sewing machine, at the beginning of the twentieth century. This method is an excellent way to produce intricate geometric shapes. Provided the component strips of fabric and their seam allowances are kept dead accurate, the angles will be true and the corners crisp. The sketches below and opposite show how the chequer-board design was worked out.

1   Cut three strips of white moiré and three of black silk, each measuring 94 x 11 cm/37 x 4½ in. These dimensions include 6 mm/¼ in seam allowances. Machine-stitch the strips so that the colours alternate (see sketch below). Press, pushing the seams under the black strips.

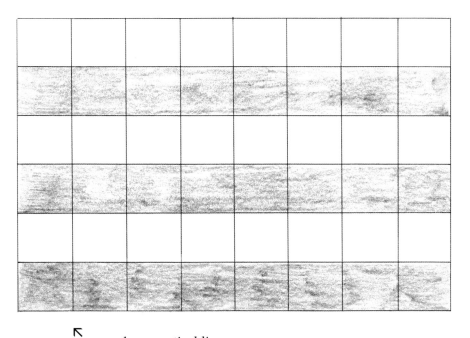

↖ cut along vertical lines

The sketch on the right shows how the chequer-board pattern, used for Seminole Abstractions *on page 99, is arrived at. Bands of fabric of equal width are first machine-stitched together. The vertical lines show where the fabric is then cut, producing new strips.*

Look at the sketch above and, starting from the left edge, measure 11 cm/4½ in. These measurements once again include 6 mm/¼ in seam allowances. Draw a line using a quilting pencil and repeat until you've marked eight strips of equal width. Cut along those lines and trim off the excess fabric at the end of the piece. Arrange the strips on the table and create the chequer-board. Pin and machine-stitch, making sure that the corners are accurate. Press. The result will look like the sketch on the page opposite, with surplus squares along two sides (marked with a cross on the sketch).

← hanging →

This sketch shows how the cut strips have been arranged to form a chequer-board. The surplus squares, marked with a cross, must then be unpicked carefully so as not to damage the seam allowance, leaving an oblong made up of 8 x 5 squares (see finished hanging on page 99).

2 Unpick the redundant squares, making sure you keep the seam allowance intact. Press and line the piece with cotton lawn.

3 Make a circular template, 5.5 cm/2^1/$_4$ in in diameter. Trace this circle very lightly at the centre of a few white squares, using a pale grey quilting pencil. It is better to mark a few at a time as the pencil tends to fade. Set the machine for free-motion embroidery or for straight stitching (whichever you prefer) and go over the circle once, using black thread and making sure the drawn line is covered. Then go over this line two more times, but more freely, so that it no longer looks so perfectly 'drawn'. Set the fagotting stitch and go over the circle yet again, then criss-cross it inside as shown. This creates an interesting, spiky pattern. Do not make every circle the same; vary the angle of the criss-crossing lines and their density. A *shisha* is then attached at the edge of the circle, using silver-grey rayon thread. Seven single daisy stitches radiate outwards from the *shisha*. A tiny spider is

If you want to make a piece in a different size or vary the pattern, while still using the seminole method, spend a little time on preparation and make sketches to work out the number of strips required to produce the pattern of your choice. This will save time and avoid wasting fabric.

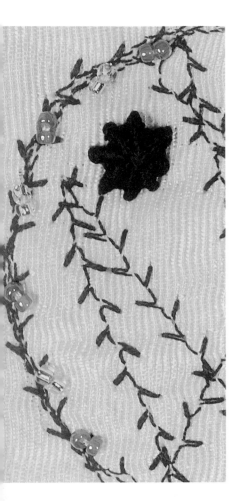

Detail of embroidered motif, showing the red spider and the beading.

Opposite page. Seminole Abstractions measures 90 x 59 cm/35¹/₂ x 23¹/₄ in. Photographed by Sarah Dewe. I was so delighted with this piece that I decided to make three cushions to complement it. See page 121.

embroidered opposite the *shisha* – the red being carefully chosen to tone with the red of the prairie points that outline the edge of the patchwork. Alternate pairs of tiny silver and pale grey glass beads outline the circle. Add a single larger silver bead over a silver sequin (see detail opposite).

4   Make a diamond and a triangular template and draw them over the black circles, using a white quilting pencil and varying their angle from square to square. Go over the outline, using the fagotting stitch, working one shape in white and the other in silver thread. Press.

5   Measure the finished piece and cut an oblong of domett and the same of cotton lawn so that they extend 5.5 cm/2¹/₄ in all around the patchwork. Place lawn face down with the domett on top, then centre the patchwork uppermost, making sure the margins are even. Baste/tack the layers at close intervals. Using silver thread, machine-quilt the patchwork 'in the ditch'.

6   For the prairie points, you'll need 84 pieces of red silk, each 4 cm/1⁵/₈ in square. Using a hot iron, fold them twice diagonally to make small triangles with all the raw edges at the base. Pin each point in position, starting from the middle of one long side, making sure they point towards the centre.

7   Measure the shorter dimensions of the piece and cut two strips of white moiré to that length and 14 cm/5¹/₂ in wide. Pin to the edge of the patchwork, over the prairie points, and machine-stitch. Press down. Repeat for the two long sides. Fold the fabric over the edge of the domett along the two short sides to form the borders; turn the raw edge under, and attach it to the back of the hanging. Repeat for the long sides, mitring the corners.

8   Line the back of the piece with an oblong of strong calico. When I was working this piece, I then machine-quilted the border, stitching 6 mm/¹/₄ in away from the edge of the patchwork, using silver thread.

9   The piece will look equally good hung upright, as shown opposite, or landscape. If you decide to hang it landscape, it could look very nice hung from a series of short loops, made to the same width as the squares. In this case, I used the invisible ring-and-batten method for hanging the piece (see page 124).

Fragments

A chance meeting with the mosaicist, Elaine M. Goodwin, left me with the mental picture of a fragment of tiled floor in the grass. I felt that the old English technique of tumbling blocks, which creates a *trompe l'oeil* effect often used in classical floors, was a good candidate for what I wanted to achieve. The detail shown below left is from the first picture in this series. It has 'clumps' of long-and-short hand embroidery, highlighted with beading, and encroaching upon the blocks. I also wanted to incorporate a stylized leaf shape. This would be left as a negative pattern, while the background of the piece would be filled with free-hand machine embroidery. I have always been fascinated by the 'tumbling block' technique, and enjoy using its traditional character in a novel setting, combining it with hand and machine embroidery and beading.

SUPPLIES

- One oblong each of white moiré and of fine cotton lawn, each 64 x 46 cm/29 x 18 in (this allows for an extra 10 cm/4 in all around the work, for framing)
- Silks and cottons for tumbling blocks
- DMC rayon hand-embroidery threads; Madeira metallic, and Natesh machine-embroidery threads
- Glass beads
- *Shishas*

1 The three pieces shown on this spread are worked in the same manner. The tumbling block panel (see page 60 for basic method and template) is worked first. It is pinned over the background fabric, which is first lined with cotton lawn. Run a line of basting/tacking around the tumbling block motif to mark its position. (It is easier to work on the background before the tumbling blocks are attached, as their thickness can interfere with the embroidery frame.) Also run a line of tacking/basting to outline the edges of the work (64 x 35½ cm/25 x 14 in).

2 Position the leaf templates over the background as desired and trace lightly around them, using a quilting pencil. Position the *shishas* and plan any hand embroidery motifs. Mark their positions.

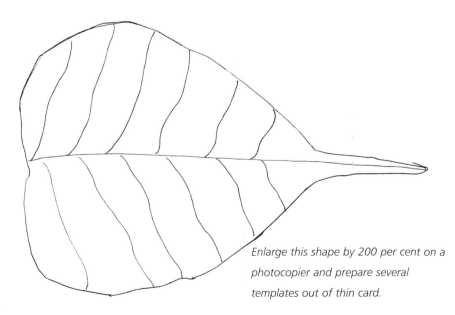

Enlarge this shape by 200 per cent on a photocopier and prepare several templates out of thin card.

3 Stitch the leaf shapes, using a silver metallic embroidery thread, in free-hand machine embroidery. Set the machine to straight sewing. It requires a little practice to follow the drawn outline accurately, but this gives a much smoother effect than trying to do it with the machine foot in place.

4 Attach *shishas* and work hand embroidery. Cover the background with free-hand machine embroidery, using crazy stitch in the density of your choice. Slip-stitch the blocks, and press. Attach beads, and press again.

The pieces shown on this spread are framed under glass, and it is interesting to see the development of the design. The unframed pieces of embroidery measure 64 x 35½ cm/25 x 14 in. Detail on opposite page.

Note. The leaf shape used for the motif is that of the *peepul* tree *(Ficus religiosa)*. This tree is very ancient and is regarded as sacred in India, where its trunk is often surrounded by flowers and offerings at roadside shrines. Its vast branches and dense foliage often harbour family groups of Indian rhesus monkeys which are protected as the representatives of Hanuman, the monkey-faced god. The Buddha is also said to have achieved enlightenment while sitting in the shade of such a tree at Budh Gaya in northern India. The leaves are beautifully shaped (see dried specimens used in *Serenity* on page 115). The skeletons of the leaf are strong and flexible, and I have used them extensively (see pages 111 and 113, for example).

Lost Continent

This piece is a natural development from the design idea used for *Fragments* (see pages 100–101). The 'continent' is made up of 56 blocks (see page 60 for basic method and template).

SUPPLIES

- 137 x 71 cm/54 x 28 in of raw silk
- Three oblongs of cotton lawn and one of domett, the same size as the silk
- Raw silks, jacquard silk, cottons, and moiré for the blocks
- DMC rayon hand-embroidery threads; Madeira metallic, and Natesh machine-embroidery threads
- Hand-quilting thread to match background silk
- Specimen beads
- 52 *shishas*

1   Line the piece of background silk and mark its outer limits with a line of basting/tacking.

2   Choose a colour scheme for the tumbling blocks. I used colours that I had observed in precious marble floors in Venice, in which the pieces had been cut in complicated geometric shapes, creating elaborate visual illusions. It is worth spending time arranging the fabrics with care to obtain pleasing and arresting combinations. I needed 168 paper templates to produce 56 finished blocks.

3   Assemble the blocks and baste/tack the panel over the lined background. Also run a line of basting/tacking close to the tumbling block motif to mark its position. It is much easier working on the background before the tumbling blocks are attached – their thickness makes it difficult to tighten the embroidery frame. The motif will therefore be removed from the background once the *shisha* work is completed and when you are ready to start on the machine embroidery. The tacked/basted outline will nevertheless remind you of the exact position of the tumbling block motif.

4   Position all the *shishas* on the work. Stand well back and look at the effect. Mark their positions lightly with a quilting pencil. Embroider them in place, choosing your colours carefully to complement the blocks nearest to them.

5   Remove the tumbling block patchwork and start work on the upper border, which is free-motion embroidered (see detail on pages 48–49). I worked in an up-and-down motion, keeping the speed fairly low and using the lighter thread first, leaving plenty of space around this initial round of stitching.   Repeat all along the border, working within the marked area of the piece. Repeat with the other two threads. Imagine that you are doodling with a pencil! Embroider the bottom border in the same manner, but keep it narrower. Press.

6   Pin the motif in position and slip-stitch to the background. Place one of the remaining oblongs of lawn on the table, then the domett and, finally, lay the piece on top. Pin or baste/tack it all over to hold the layers together. Run a line of hand-quilting ¼ in/6 mm away from the tumbling block motif.

Opposite page. Lost Continent *measures 131 x 66 cm/51½ x 26 in.*

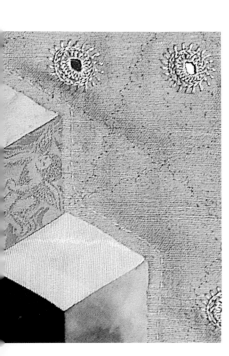

Opposite. Adrift *measures*
131 x 63 cm/51½ x 25 in.

7 I used one of the fancy automatic stitches and a transparent embroidery foot to run delicate lines of machine stitchery, worked almost tone on tone, all over the background of the piece (see detail on the left). Attach specimen beads.

8 Turn over the raw edges of the piece. Press. Slip-stitch edges to the back of the work. Line the hanging with the remaining oblong of lawn. Prepare a sleeve for the hanging pole. (It is better if the latter is kept narrow and thin – provided it is rigid – so that it does not make the border curl around too much.) Fix your personalized label.

Adrift

The piece shown on the page opposite was worked very much in the same way as *Lost Continent*, yet it is quite different. I wonder if I am finally out of my tumbling-block phase! I used a creamy slub silk behind the motif, and the borders and simple background stitchery were replaced by a great swathe of free-hand machine embroidery (see detail on page 61).

The background fabric was cut to its exact size, 131 x 63 cm/51½ x 25 in, with the addition of a 6mm/¼ in seam allowance all around.

Work the machine embroidery. Slip-stitch the motif back on. Prepare the lawn/domett/patchwork 'sandwich', and baste/tack all over. Do not quilt around the motifs but attach tiny glass beads at the intersection of each block. Distribute these also over the machine-embroidered area, choosing beads to tone with the thread. Make sure to go right through the layers as you stitch the beads. This in effect quilts the hanging. Remove basting/tacking, and press.

Cut two strips of cream silk, 6 cm/2½ in wide, to the length of the long dimensions of the piece. Pin and machine-stitch 6 mm/¼ in from the edge. Cut the ends of the seam at an angle; press, and turn raw edge under. Slip-stitch. Repeat for short dimensions.

Hand-quilt the edges of the hanging, stitching 2 cm/¾ in away from the edges. Press. Fix the final backing. For hanging, I used the rings-and-batten method (see page 124). Attach your personalized label.

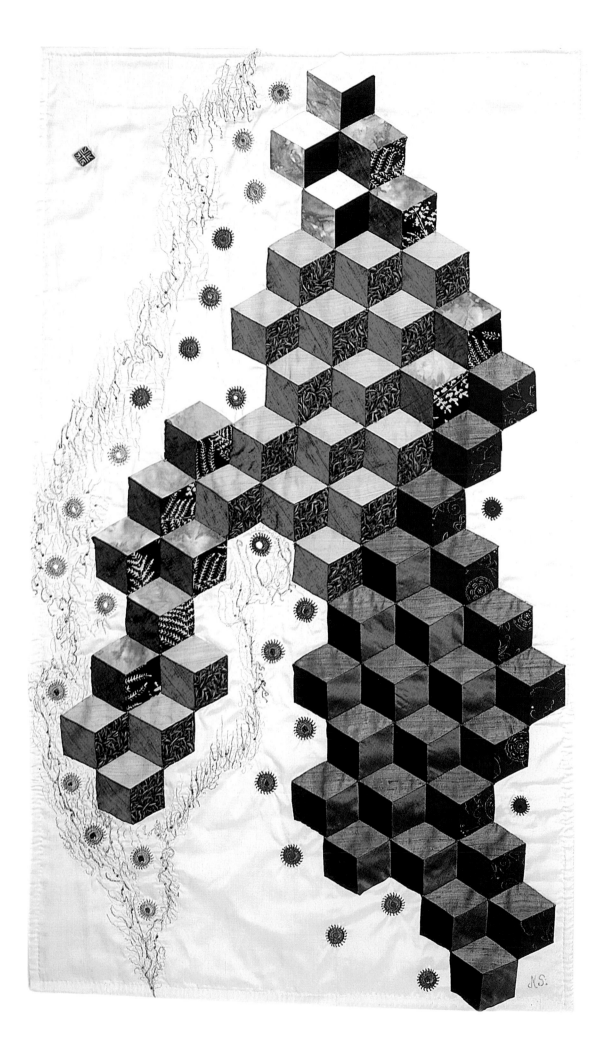

The Sea, the Sea

SUPPLIES

- 97 x 24 cm/38 x 9½ in of synthetic slub taffeta or other man-made fabric (transfer dyes do not work well on pure cotton or silk)
- Three oblongs of cotton lawn, one of domett and one of white non-absorbent paper, all the same size as the taffeta
- DMC rayon hand embroidery threads; Güttermann and Madeira smooth and metallic machine embroidery threads
- *Shishas*
- Chinese enamelled beads, small glass bead.
- One pot each of transfer fabric paints in blue, pink, mauve, sage green and grey
- Small piece of sponge

The American art-quilt artist, Libby Lehman, writes in one of her books that although she loves the subtlety of hand-dyed fabrics, she has no desire to dye them herself! 'Part of the reason quiltmaking first appealed to me,' she says, 'was that it did not smell and my hands stayed dry – the antithesis of dyeing.' I'm afraid I rather suffer from the same prejudice, and I'm always very appreciative when one of my textile-artist friends donates some of her precious scraps to me, as in *Blue Window* on page 75.

This small wallhanging is therefore very much a departure from my normal principles, but I enjoyed doing it as it was not so much dying as painting, or rather sponging, colour on to paper. This means that it can be discarded if you are not happy with the initial result. You can also work on a larger piece of paper and select the best area. The transfer colours are sponged on to the paper in a free-flowing pattern, allowing the colours to blend into each other. Allow the paper to dry and iron on the fabric (make sure to check the manufacturer's instructions). On a synthetic fabric the colours will be deep and vibrant, whereas they turn rather pallid on pure cotton or silk, hence the advice on fabric choice.

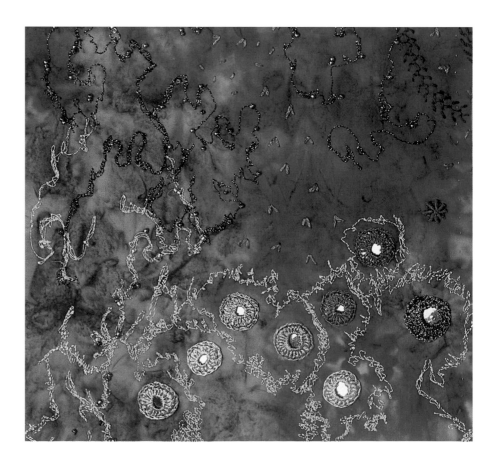

Right. Detail from the hanging The Sea, the Sea.

Opposite page. The Sea, the Sea *measures 92 x 20 cm/36¼ x 8 in.*

From the outset, I wanted this hanging to have depth of colour and to suggest the bottom of the sea. A trip to the amazing Bead Shop in London had yielded some beautiful Chinese enamel beads, some of them starfish-shaped. A friend with a passion for the late Iris Murdoch's novels took one look at the piece, which I had just completed, and exclaimed: 'The Sea, the Sea'. Life has these little moments!

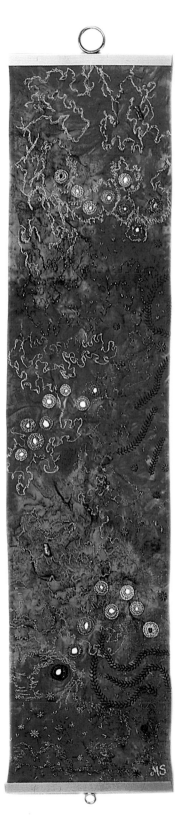

1 The painted fabric is lined with fine cotton lawn in the usual manner. Run a line of basting/tacking to mark the final dimensions of the piece. The *shishas* are positioned and embroidered in carefully gradated colours. Next, work the machine embroidery and finally, the hand-embroidered details: curving lengths of feather stitch, spiders to complement the *shishas*, and a variety of speckling stitches.

2 When the machine and the hand embroidery are complete, lay one of the remaining pieces of lawn face down on the table, and cover it with the domett. Trim these two layers to the finished size of the piece. Centre the embroidered piece over the domett, and distribute the small glass beads over the machine embroidery. Attach the specimen beads, using quilting thread. While beading, make sure that the thread goes through all the layers of fabric.

3 I found the solid brass 'bell-pull' fitting in London, though it was imported from Denmark. If you want to use this kind of fitting, buy it first and let its width dictate that of the hanging.

4 Turn over the raw edges of the long sides and slip-stitch them to the back of the work.

5 If you are using a similar bell-pull fitting, trim the top and bottom end of the piece, along the basted/tacked line. Stay-stitch very close to the edge and neaten with a row of zigzag stitches. If you are unable to obtain a suitable fitting, the piece can be hung by the rings-and-batten method (see page 124). In this case, the top and bottom edges should be turned over in the same way as the long ones. You may then also decide to weigh down the piece with a few attractive specimen beads, fixed to the bottom edge.

6 Hand-quilt the long sides of the hanging, close to the edge. Use the remaining oblong of lawn to line the back. Attach to the bell-pull fitting, if applicable, and slip-stitch your personalized label.

Crooked Paths

The previous piece, *The Sea, the Sea*, combined *shisha* work and machine embroidery in a meandering pattern that complemented the painted background. *Crooked Paths* was assembled in exactly the same way as *The Sea, the Sea*. The background was a beautiful piece of moiré fabric. The outlines of the naïve stars were traced lightly with a quilting pencil and machine embroidered, using a rich turquoise metallic thread.

Crooked Paths was suggested by some lines from a poem by the great Spanish poet, Antonio Machado:

> *Caminante, son tus huellas*
> *el camino, y nada más*
> *Caminante no hay camino,*
> *Se hace el camino al andar…*
>
> *Caminante, no hay camino,*
> *sino estelas en la mar.*

> Wanderer, your footsteps
> are the path, and nothing else.
> Wanderer, there is no path
> You make the path as you tread it…
>
> Wanderer, there is no path,
> except for the memory of your footsteps
> on the sea.

The trail of *shisha* work is echoed by the meandering line of feather stitch. Small clumps of hand embroidery, composed of spiders and little stars, are balanced by specimen beads.

Simplicity

This small piece is made of raw shot grey silk. It uses a lot of *kantha* quilting, which you will also see in the coming section.

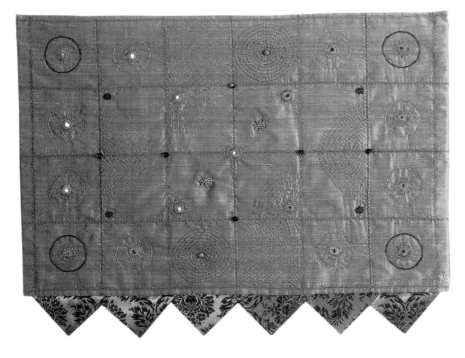

Above. A detail from Crooked Paths, *124 x 21 cm/ 48³/₄ x 8¹/₄ in, showing the juxtaposition of free-motion machined stars and of hand embroidery. The whole piece is shown on the page opposite.*

Left. Simplicity *measures 47 x 63 cm/18¹/₂ x 25 in.*

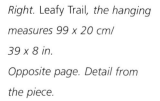

Leafy Trail

SUPPLIES

- 107 x 28 cm/42 x 11 in of hand-woven shot silk
- Three oblongs of fine lawn and one of domett, the same size as the silk
- Six *peepul* skeleton leaves
- DMC rayon and red metallic hand-embroidery threads
- Four specimen beads to weight the bottom of the piece

Right. Leafy Trail, *the hanging measures 99 x 20 cm/ 39 x 8 in.*
Opposite page. Detail from the piece.

This piece combines *kantha* quilting, *shisha* work and fragile-looking real *peepul* leaf skeletons (see the note on this tree and the place it occupies in Hindu/Buddhist iconography on page 101). The skeleton remaining after the chlorophyll has been extracted from the leaves is extremely dense and flexible. These skeletons are now easily available in craft shops. For centuries they were used in India as a background for painted miniatures, usually of religious subjects. These are still produced today, but you are more likely to come across hand-made greeting cards produced by this method – not so fine but more affordable!

1   I discovered that I could stitch right through the skeletons, using a fine silver thread. Alternatively, they can be stuck to the piece with fabric adhesive. I sometimes brush them lightly with gold, using fabric paint. Some of the leaves may be slightly concave, but a quick press with a steam iron will soon correct this. The steam also improves the flexibility of the leaves if they have spent a long time in a drawer.

2   This piece was worked and assembled in exactly the same way as *The Sea, the Sea* on page 106. Use the rings-and-batten method to hang the piece (see page 124).

3   For obvious reasons, I keep the actual fixing of the leaves to the background as the penultimate operation – immediately before lining the back of the work. To have a guideline for the double rows of *kantha* quilting around the leaves, cut paper templates of the leaf skeletons, baste/tack these to the cloth and embroider around them.

Entrapped Leaves

These two pieces combine leaf skeletons and *kantha* quilting to create a feeling of inner peace and tranquillity. The quilting follows concentric patterns, as in a *mandala*. The background of each piece is divided in a ruler-drawn grid, and then embroidered in silver thread with the fagotting stitch on the machine (a satin stitch would also look attractive but would be heavier). Start by lining the silk with lawn, as usual. Baste/tack a line to mark the actual size of the finished piece. Press.

SUPPLIES

- 75 x 55cm/29 x 22 in of thick écru raw silk
- Three oblongs of fine lawn and one of domett, the same size as the silk
- 12 *peepul* skeleton leaves
- DMC rayon and metallic hand embroidery threads; Madeira oxidized silver metallic machine embroidery thread
- 1 m/40 in of oxidized silver cord
- *Shishas*
- Small mother-of-pearl button

1   For the piece shown below, measure the top and bottom, find the centre and make a mark, top and bottom. Using a ruler and a pale grey quilting pencil, draw a line down the middle and fill the piece of silk with lines 9 cm/3½ in apart. Repeat across the width. Embroider the lines. Press.

2   Refer to the photograph to see how the *kantha* quilting was carried out. When stitching concentric shapes, always start from the centre or from the corner of the square, fanning outwards. The lines of quilting are worked 6 mm/¼ in apart. For the couched coils of silver cord, flatten the end of the cord. Stitch it firmly to the top of the background fabric and start coiling the cord over the raw end, attaching the growing coil with small stitches as you go along. The central motifs, embroidered in chain stitch in dark pink, are based on a traditional design (see page 43 for a similar motif).

For the leaf treatment and the assembly of the piece, follow steps 1 to 3, page 110.

The piece on the opposite page is made of heavy white silk. The grid forms diamonds, and the leaves are brushed lightly with gold and fixed with fabric adhesive, instead of being sewn on. The piece was framed with narrow borders made of old pink silk.

Right. Detail of Entrapped Leaves *measures 65 x 47 cm/ 25¾ x 18¾ in.*

Opposite page. Entrapped Leaves II *measures 61½ x 48 cm/24¼ x 19 in.*

Serenity

SUPPLIES

- An oblong of deep écru thick raw silk and one of cotton lawn, each 117½ x 37½ cm/46¼ x 14¾ in
- Closely woven fabric to cover the front of the board, form a border and turn under
- DMC rayon hand embroidery threads in brown, pale yellow and a deeper shade; Madeira machine embroidery thread in red, and Natesh in clear gold
- Small pearls, a few copper-coloured embroidery glass beads
- 14 *shishas*
- 3 large dry *peepul* leaves (replace by attractive dried leaves if unavailable)
- Oblong of MDF and one of domett, cut to the size of the finished embroidery, allowing for a 4 cm/1½ in border all around

Back to *peepul* leaves! On previous pages you will find pieces in which I have used the skeletons of these leaves, as I am fascinated by the beauty of their shapes and their iconographic significance (see page 101). The skeleton leaves are now widely available in western countries, though not the dry ones – unless you have a good friend working inside the tropical hot house at a botanical garden! I discovered the three perfectly preserved specimens, brought back from a trip home, inside a long-unopened book. Summer or autumn maple leaves would also look wonderful, or you could have a scatter of the fan-shaped ginkgo leaves. The ginkgo (*Ginkgo biloba*) is a similarly ancient tree, with classical Chinese and Japanese literary connotations.

1   Line the silk with cotton lawn as usual. Stay-stitch the edges and run a zigzag over them. Although this stitch is meant to prevent fraying, use a matching thread so that it does not show when you come to satin-stitch the edge to finish off the piece (see step 7). Press.

2   With a ruler and a pencil, trace the outer lines of the border, 3 cm/1¼ in from the edge of the fabric. Draw the inner rectangle 4 cm/1½ in inside the existing lines. Starting from the left-hand side of the long side of the border, mark thirteen square sections. Start again from the opposite side of the same length of border, and draw another thirteen sections. You should end up with a rectangular cartouche at the center on each side (see detail reproduced on the top of page 115). The shorter sides of the embroidery have six square sections, with a larger cartouche in the center.

3   Set the machine for straight stitch and free-motion embroidery. First go three times over the outer and inner lines of the border to cover the drawn line completely. Then stitch several times around those squares that will be filled with a greater density of embroidery. Start filling these squares, quite slowly, allowing the needle to form small rounded shapes and leaving a rough circle in the center. Cross over to the next square with a row of meandering stitches (see detail on the left-hand page and the finished piece, right).

4   Use the gold thread to hand-stitch over the densely embroidered squares. Keep the thread lengths short to prevent breakage – machine thread is not meant to be used for hand embroidery, but I like its delicacy. Use a fine needle and do not draw the thread too tight. Work a tracery of running stitches, converging in the center of the square (see detail). Finish off with a tiny pearl stitched in the middle. The corner squares each have a *shisha* in the middle, worked in brown

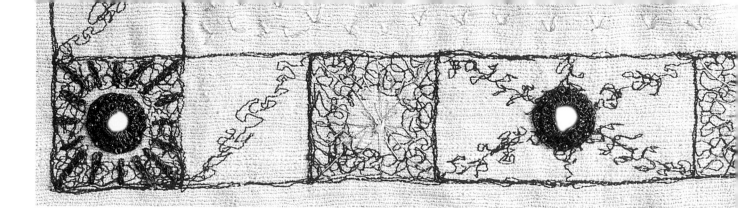

DMC rayon thread and decorated with tiny copper-coloured embroidery beads. Radiating lines of chain stitch complete the motifs. Work the rectangular cartouches. Press.

5 Trace the outline of each leaf on paper. Cut out and baste/tack these templates down the centre of the piece. Determine the position of the two groups of three *shishas* and work them in dark yellow.

6 Fill the background with small filling stitches, using pale yellow thread and varying the angles of the stitches. Stop a short distance from the leaf outlines and the *shishas*.

7 Set the machine for satin stitch, reducing the upper tension if necessary, and go over the previously worked zigzag edge. You may have to do this twice to obtain a really dense and chunky edge. Press.

8 Fix the oblong of domett to the front of the board, using fabric adhesive. Baste/tack the embroidered panel to the centre of the fabric selected to cover the board, ensuring that the embroidery is as square as possible. Slip-stitch close to the satin-stitched edge. Stretch the piece over the board, centring the embroidery. Trim the edges of the fabric so that they overlap those of the board by 7¹/₂ cm/3 in. (Remember to add the thickness of the board to this measurement.) Lace the back as shown below.

Diagrams *a* and *b* show the stages of lacing both sides of the fabric over the board. The corners are then mitred as shown in *c*.

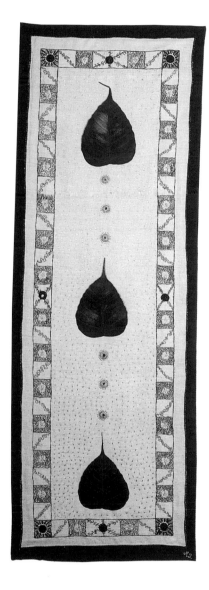

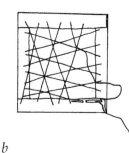

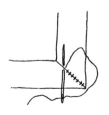

a 　　　　　　*b* 　　　　　　*c*

Serenity, 122 x 44 cm/ 48¹/4 x 17¹/2 in; the hanging was finally stretched over a piece of board, see step 8, left.

Cushion-making

To ensure that your cushion looks well filled, the inner pad should always be slightly larger than its cover. For instance, the cushion cover shown on the opposite page measures 43⅕ cm/17 in square, and contains a cushion pad 45 cm/18 in square.

I love cushions! When I go to someone's house I first inspect their books, and then the cushions fall under my scrutiny. Lovingly plumped up or rumpled into the back of the sofa, they tell a lot about their owners – or so I think.

By and large, I prefer them without a zip. Of course, this may not be practical if they are light in colour. Many people prefer to have a zip, as they find the prospect of unpicking and sewing the opening by hand daunting. Yet unless you have toddlers and/or a houseful of dogs, cushions do not get dirty that quickly. Therefore, the machine-embroidered strip patchwork cushions shown on page 59 do not have a zip. They are also simple to finish as they are not piped or corded around the edges. To make them just that little bit more special, however, I attached an attractive specimen bead at each corner, before putting in the pad and closing the opening. The beads must be really firmly attached. Use a double thickness of buttonhole thread and stitch them like buttons, pushing a pin under the bead, as the needle goes through the holes, to keep the bead away from the corner of the cushion. Go through the holes several times, then wind the thread firmly round and round under the bead so that it stands proud in its corner. Knot the thread securely. Insert the pad inside the prepared cover, and slip-stitch the opening carefully, so that the stitches are barely visible.

A word about pads. Do not be tempted to buy one filled with bits of plastic foam or loosely filled with feathers. It is important that the pad is really plump and filled with good-quality feathers, even though the cushion will not be used as a pillow. Only good-quality feathers will keep their loft and ensure that your beautiful cushion does not end up all rumpled in the back of the sofa! For the same reason, the pad should always be slightly larger than its cover. Pads come in a variety of sizes, and it is a good idea to buy the pad before you start out on the cushion.

The cushion shown on the opposite page does not have a zip either. The metallic silk incorporated in the design is bright, but its texture does not attract dirt. The back is made of crushed black velvet. I always try to give unexpected backs to my cushions, joining fabrics of two different colours diagonally, or using an interesting fabric.

This cushion has a strip patchwork panel (see method on page 58) surrounded by large borders made of thick brown raw silk. These borders are machine-embroidered in a simple chevron pattern, worked in fagotting stitch with Güttermann gold thread. Instead of beads, I attached large home-made tassels at the corners. These are fun to make, besides being much cheaper than commercially produced ones, and you can match colours exactly. For these I used brown chenille, mixed with matt yellow crochet cotton and a lurex yarn. The sketches below show how to make them.

First cut a cardboard template to the size of the eventual tassel and tie the yarn around it, then proceed as shown in the diagrams.

a
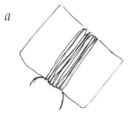

b
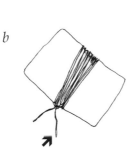

c

Slide a piece of yarn under the threads, as shown, and then tie it securely.

Cut yarn along here.

Wind a length of yarn around the top to form the head of the tassel.

Left. Medieval Cushion, *43.5 cm/17 in.*

A word about borders. The cushion on the previous page had a panel surrounded by borders. I use this formula a lot, as it highlights the embroidery or other work so that it stands out. The embroidery does not rub on the sofa and therefore lasts longer. It also means that you can afford to be much more elaborate in the panel, as you're working on a smaller surface instead of covering the entire front of the cushion. The sketches below show the assembly order for the following: a – a square cushion; b – a rectangular cushion; c – one with inset corners, of the type shown on the opposite page (bottom); and d – a cushion with a double log cabin border, like the pair shown below.

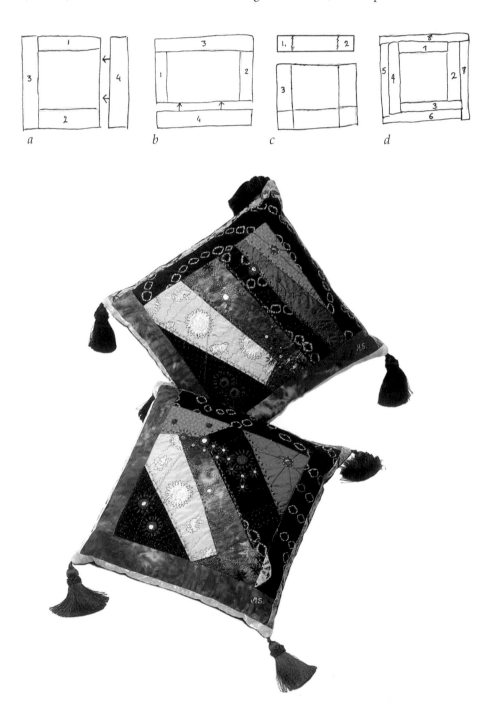

Right. This pair of cushions was made to tone up with the Indian Spring Memories *hanging, reproduced on page 69. They each measure 43½ cm/17 in square. They are backed with fine blue cord and trimmed with commercially bought tassels.*

Opposite. The two floor cushions measure 62 cm/24½ in square. They are backed with blue moiré fabric and have a zip in the middle of the back.

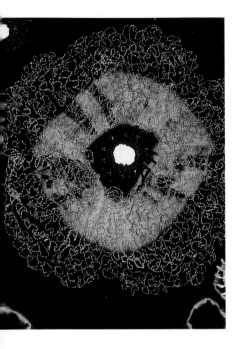

The *shisha* work used on the floor cushions shown on the previous page is a good example of an interesting fabric suggesting the embroidery. I had bought a length of pure cotton damask, tied-and-dyed in indigo, and used it for the borders and the sashing of the large *Indian Spring Memories* hanging (see page 69). The fabric came from Guinea and was the kind of African textile used for the men's traditional robes. In the same way as I used the eyes of the tie-and-dye as a guide to hand-quilting in the hanging, I decided to emphasize the pattern with *shishas*. The centre of the dyed pattern became a flower, with delicate free-motion machine embroidery, radiating from a central *shisha*. A close-up of this detail is shown on the left.

Above. Detail of a machine-embroidered flower at the centre of a cushion.

Because I use delicate silk fabrics, I seek to lessen the pressure put on seams even by the normal use of the cushion – a cushion is a functional item and you shouldn't have to worry about using it! By adding a layer of cotton lawn to the completed fronts and backs of my cushion, then assembling them as if they were two single pieces of fabric, the cushion will crease less and is unlikely to split along the seams.

The group of cushions opposite was made to complement the *Seminole Abstractions* hanging, reproduced on page 99. They have piped edges, outlining narrow red silk borders as in sketch *a*, on page 118. If you want to make these cushions, refer to the explanations for the hanging, the only difference being that the squares are smaller. Each cushion is made up of 25 squares, each square measuring 9.2 cm/3¾ in (inclusive of seams). The chequer-board is framed by a narrow border, 3.6 cm/1½ in. Make yourself a sketch to calculate the number of strips you will need to cut for the seminole patchwork, as this will depend on the size and shape of the cushion. I used the round motif for the embroidery and omitted the beading. The centre squares have *shishas* worked in red to match the silk of the borders. One cushion is backed in black silk, the other in red and the third, as already mentioned, is cut diagonally – one half black and the other red.

a   45° angle

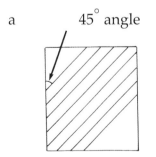

Cutting bias strips for a cushion.

b

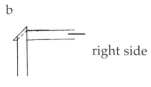

right side

Joining bias strips.

Piped edges are an elegant and professional way of finishing a cushion. Piping gets plenty of wear and tear, so instead of the black slub silk used in the patchwork, I used an inexpensive synthetic – a black, closely-woven fabric – from which to cut the required bias strips. You'll need a square metre/yard of fabric, and the strips must be cut at a 45 degree angle, see sketch *a*, left. They are then joined together to form a continuous length (see sketch *b*). Strips 4 cm/1½ in wide will accommodate most thicknesses of piping cord, which is sold by the metre/yard.

Fit a piping or a zipper foot on the sewing machine (consult your manual). Cut a length of bias strip. Insert the piping cord. Start at the centre of one side and machine-stitch as close as possible to the cord. Clip the bias strip as it goes round the corner. It looks better if the piping curves gently round the corner, rather than being applied at right angles.

An alternative to piping is the special decorative cord which comes with a flat edge. This is then hidden in the seam once the cord is attached round the cushion. It is applied very much like piping: using the piping or zipper foot on your machine, start to sew in the centre of one side and stitch as close to the actual cord as you can. The tumbling block cushion, on the left of the picture reproduced on page 60, is trimmed with this type of green cord.

Below. The three cushion covers, each measuring 43.5 cm/17½ in square, are all made from embroidered seminole patchwork. Photographed by Curtis Lane & Co.

Wallhangings and Framed Pictures – Presentation and Conservation

I am fanatical about the presentation of my work. I really think that if one has spent three hundred hours producing something, it deserves to be framed or hung as well as can possibly be managed. I have gone to exhibitions so many times and seen an innovative, gorgeous piece of work hanging from the proverbial garden cane or crammed in a frame that is not the right size because it came from a kit and, like every kit in the world, this only came in a narrow range of sizes. Even a great painting can be marred by an ill-chosen frame, while a so-so work can be made to look much more attractive if carefully mounted and framed. Too many textile artists ignore or disregard this simple fact.

Framed or unframed? By and large, I prefer my textiles unframed, although many people worry about the piece getting dirty. I'm always puzzled by this. For centuries people have had tapestries, rugs, bed hangings and so on in rooms that were lit with candles and heated by open fires. Yet many of these extraordinary textiles are still around for us to admire. Indeed Egyptian, amazing pre-Colombian textiles and many others have survived entombed, their bright colours and richness revealed by modern-day archeologists. But if you must frame it, then treat your work as you would a precious painting. Have it done professionally, and don't skimp on the size of the frame or mount. The embroidery should never touch the glass and the framer must introduce a filet, which is a tiny slice of wood, finished to match the frame and fitted inside it to hold the work away from the glass.

If the work is to be framed, make sure that you leave at least a 10 cm/4 in margin all around it to enable the framer to fix it over a board. If the piece was completed without margins and you decide at a later stage to have it framed, mount it over a piece of calico, with margins as described above. Choose a high-quality picture framer, who will hold a large selection of framing strips and mounts and advise you as to the best treatment for your work. Going to exhibitions, I see how so many textile artists invariably present their work framed in unfinished wood. This relatively cheap and informal option looks fine next to unframed textiles or others that are similarly framed. It will, however, look pretty silly opposite a painting in a formal frame and in a room filled with period furniture. Look at your work carefully and consider the decor before making a decision.

A good way to present work is to block it. This can be done professionally or you can do it yourself. A panel of MDF can be used, but I tend to cover this with museum-

This is an example of the type of work which looks best when framed under glass. Homage to Kandinski *is made of silk chiffon appliquéd on raw silk. The edges of the work were finished off with a narrow satin stitch. I gave some of the thread to the framer, who used it to attach the work to the board with a few stitches. He then added a gold filet to match the frame and keep the glass away from the work. Remember that if you want to sign your work, this is done on the board or mount and you'll need to do this once the framer has cut these and before he fits the glass.*

quality board, as the wood amalgamate is full of chemicals that may damage your work in the long run. I leave a sufficient cloth margin around the piece to enable me to wrap it around the edges of the board, then lace the work at the back, see page 115. After this, I attach a piece of calico to hide the back and two rings to hang the work. If, however, as in the case of *Serenity* shown on the same page, I decide to block the piece at a later stage and do not have a sufficient margin around the work, I first slip-stitch it to a suitable background fabric and then mount it.

My favourite method is to hang textiles from a pole or from an invisible wooden batten fixed at the back. For a pole, I buy wooden dowelling and I like this to be quite thick. This enables me to make a feature of the rounded shape of the pole inside the sleeve or channel of the hanging (see *Summer Fever* on page 77, where the channel at the top of the hanging is a continuation of the piece and is quilted). The thick sturdy pole (2.5 cm/1 in diameter) creates a nice curve which catches the light on the silk. Normally, the poles are cut to fit flush inside the channel, and I finish off the ends by drilling holes into them and fitting decorative knobs or finials. For *Summer Fever*, I used ceramic knobs normally made to fit on Indian wooden cabinets. With

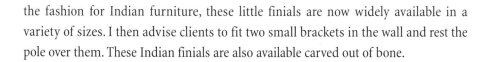

the fashion for Indian furniture, these little finials are now widely available in a variety of sizes. I then advise clients to fit two small brackets in the wall and rest the pole over them. These Indian finials are also available carved out of bone.

Lost Continent, on page 103, was hung from a heavy-duty plastic pole, 6 mm/¼ in in diameter, of the type normally used as a light pull in a bathroom. The piece has a top border that starts flush with the top of the hanging. For this reason, I wanted a thin pole which would curve the fabric as little as possible and yet be stable. The plastic is easy to cut with a hacksaw, but wear gloves when cutting as it releases small particles that can get under the skin. The diameter was far too small to drill into, but I had acquired a pair of exquisitely carved small bone finials and was anxious to use them. I tied the screw part to the pole with thick thread and then applied a strong adhesive to bind the pole and screw permanently, after which I wrapped a narrow strip of cotton fabric over the join and around the whole length of the pole to protect the inside of the channel.

Because the pole is hidden inside the sleeve, I normally leave the wood untreated. If, however, I have a piece hanging from fabric loops (see *Summer Sprites* on page 85), the pole is visible and must be sand-papered. For that piece, I used a thinner dowel, 2 cm/¾ in in diameter, and treated it with woodstain before waxing it. The pole can also be painted or sprayed to tone with the fabric of the hanging. In the case of a small piece hanging from loops, the pole can be treated as an integral part of the piece. Wrap a cotton strip around the pole to measure its diameter. Cut a strip from the main fabric used for the hanging and machine-stitch this to make a tube, slightly larger than the diameter of the pole. Slide the pole inside the tube and neatly slip-stitch the ends.

For the rings-and-batten method, stitch two small plastic curtain rings to the back of the work, and cut a piece of narrow wooden batten (2 cm/¾ in wide, 3 mm/⅛ in thick) so that it fits between them, up to the middle of the rings. Cover one side with a good quality *fabric* adhesive and press it into position. Put a few heavy books over the batten until the glue has set. See sketch below:

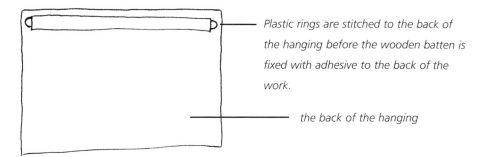

Plastic rings are stitched to the back of the hanging before the wooden batten is fixed with adhesive to the back of the work.

the back of the hanging

Because my work always consists of several layers of fabric, the adhesive never reaches the embroidered surface. It would not stain – fabric adhesives are designed to dry clear and pliable – but I always worry about the conservation angle, even though the manufacturer assures us that it is safe to use! The batten, although it is thin, keeps the work away from the wall. It is therefore less likely to collect dust and is safe from any humidity or condensation. This method only works well for relatively small pieces or those which are at least quite light. The weight of the work is taken by the sewn rings, the role of the batten being to stiffen the top of the piece and hold it nice and straight. The work may then be suspended from a short length of fishing line, which is both very strong and practically invisible, or the rings can hang from two pins fixed to the wall. If the piece is light, it can be fitted with a second piece of batten at the bottom to weigh it down.

A word about textile conservation and cleaning. I have already mentioned how most people seem terrified that some terrible calamity hovers, waiting to overcome their precious piece of textile, if it hangs unframed. As with most things, prevention is better than cure: the great enemies of your piece of work are not errant cups of coffee, but the light, central heating, dust and chemicals that lurk all around us. Of course your piece must be well lit by natural and electric light. Light is magical; it will bring your work to life and make the colours sing. How many times have you moved a picture or a rug from some area of the room and suddenly everyone comments on it and is convinced that it is new. They never noticed it because the light didn't catch it. But a balance must be reached between hanging your masterpiece in a dark corner where no one sees it, and watching its colours and texture dulling within a short period of time. A few precautions will ensure that you get the best of both worlds. Never hang a piece opposite a south-facing window – see what happens to the curtains within a few short years! A spotlight aimed at a piece of work should be kept at a safe distance from it. It is also a good idea to vary the angle of the beam from time to time. Another thing to avoid is hanging your work over a radiator or storage heater. The heat generated and the black deposit created by storage heaters are lethal to textiles. They also tend to attract dust. On the subject of dust, get into the habit of giving your hanging a little shake from time to time. A hand-held vacuum cleaner, on its lowest setting and held a short distance away from the fabric, can be useful if dust has been allowed to collect over the prominent top of a quilt or hanging, but the gentle regular shake is preferable.

I chiefly use silks in my work. I love the delicacy of colouring that can be achieved with silk and the unique way in which it catches the light. Its texture is without comparison. But it is expensive and the colours can be fugitive at times, which is why I try to give it as much protection as possible. I always line the back of the work, including quilted pieces, with an extra piece of cotton lawn or calico. This is slip-stitched in position and is therefore easily removable in case of disasters, such as water running down the wall. I believe that it would take quite a while for the water to soak through to the top of the work, due to the number of layers that I include in the making-up of a piece. Orthodox quilters are horrified by this. They think that the back of the quilt is as interesting as the front. I agree to some extent, but I design my pieces to go on the wall and not on a bed, and I'd rather protect them from possible damage in any way I can.

An excellent safe way to remove dust trapped in precious fabrics is to heat a bag of flour in the oven. Put the piece of work inside a large paper bag and pour the hot flour over the textile. Shake the bag for several minutes. Allow the flour to cool; take the textile out of the bag – preferably in the garden – and give it a good shake. You'll be amazed at the amount of dust which has stuck to the flour. The textile will be quite revived. This is particularly effective with antique lace and delicate old silks.

If a piece has become heavily soiled or stained, dry cleaning might be the only option. Go to highly reputable cleaners and discuss the piece and the materials used, to make sure that no irreparable damage is done.

Finally, enjoy your beautiful piece of work and allow it to grow old gracefully. The colours may fade slightly over time but they'll age in unison and this will not mar the beauty of the piece. Remember that precious antique Persian rugs were once aglow with colours which would now look garish to many people's eyes!

Places to visit

United States of America. The American Folk Art Museum, 45 West, 53rd Street, New York, NY 10019. Tel. 001 212 977 7170

The American Crafts Museum, 40 West 53rd Street, New York, NY 10019. Tel. 001 212 956 3535

Cooper Hewitt Museum of Design, Smithsonian Institution, 5th Avenue at 91st Street, New York, NY. Tel. 001 212 849 8400

Los Angeles County Museum of Art, 5905 Wilshire Boulevard, Los Angeles, CA 90036. Tel. 001 323 937 4230

United Kingdom. Victoria and Albert Museum, Cromwell Road, London SW7. Tel. 020 7240 2010. (*Permanent collection, textiles not normally on show can be viewed by appointment.*)

Joss Graham, Oriental Textiles, 10 Eccleston Street, London SW1. Tel. 020 7730 4370. (*The gallery regularly holds selling exhibitions of rare antique textiles and modern high-quality ones. The shop has a varied and constantly changing stock of textiles and artefacts.*)

American Museum, Claverton Manor, Bath, BA2 7BD. Tel. 01225 460 503. (*Permanent collection of early American quilts, embroidery, furnishings and also periodic special exhibitions.*)

Cartwright Hall, Lister Park, Manningham, Bradford. Tel. 01274 751 212. (*Permanent collection, textiles not normally on show can be viewed by appointment.*)

Museum and Art Gallery, 53 New Walk, Leicester LE1 7EA. Tel. 0116 255 4100

Museum of Costumes and Textiles, 51 Castle Gate, Nottingham NG1 6AT. Tel. 0115 915 3500

India. Calico Museum of Textiles, Retreat, Shahi Bagh, Ahmedabad, Gujarat

Prince of Wales Museum, M.G. Road, Fort, Mumbai, Maharastra

Jagdish and Kamla Mittal Museum 1–2–214 Gagan Mahal Road Hyderabad, Andhra Pradesh

Maharaj Sawai Man Singh II Museum, City Palace, Jaipur, Rajasthan

Crafts Museum, Bhairon Marg, Pragati Maidan, New Delhi 110001

Bharat Bhawan, Benares Hindu University, Varanasi, Uttar Pradesh

Suppliers US

National Quilting shows, which include stands hired by specialist suppliers, are a good source of unusual or imported fabrics, usually cottons./

Connecting Threads, 13118 NE 4th St, Vancouver, WA 98684. Toll-free: 800-574-6454 Website: www.connectingthreads.com (Fabrics and supplies for embroidery & quilting)

Eclectic Etc., Inc., P.O. Box 10, Willow Grove, PA 19090-0010. Tel: (215) 658-1711 Toll-free: 1-888-SHOP-ETC Fax: (215) 658-1191 E-mail: TheHeadBead@eebeads.com Website: www.eebeads.com (An impressive variety of beads)

Exotic Silks, 1959 Leghorn Mountain View, California 94043. Tel: (650) 965-7760 Toll-free: (800) 845-7455 Fax: (650) 965-0712 E-mail: silks@exoticsilks.com Website: www.exoticsilks.com (Silks of all kinds)

Fabric.com, E-mail: customercare@fabric.com Website: www.fabric.com (Online fabric seller, they have flannel, which can be used as a Domett substitute)

JoAnn, Website: www.joann.com (Source for DMC and other embroidery floss, fabrics, quilting & needle art supplies. JoAnn has stores in the lower 48 states and Alaska.)

The Pepperell Pepper Patch, 152 Main Street, PO Box 345 Pepperell, Massachusetts 01463. Tel: 978-433-3377 Toll-Free: 888-597-7771 Website: www.pppatch.com E-mail: info@pppatch.com (Shishas, crazy quilt embellishments, and embroidery supplies)

Shipwreck Beads, 2500 Mottman Road SW, Olympia, WA 98512. Toll-free: 800-950-4232 E-mail: info@shipwreckbeads.com Website: www.shipwreckbeads.com (A huge selection of beads)

Threadart.com, 13121 Louetta Rd. #125, Cypress, TX 77429. Tel: (281)-373-0230 Toll-free: 1-866-224-4088 Fax: (281) 304-1105 Website: www.threadart.com (Full range of quilting and embroidery supplies)

TREADLEART, 25834 Narbonne Ave, Lomita, CA 90717. Tel: 310-534-5122 Fax: 310-534-8372 E-mail: treadleart@treadleart.com Website: www.treadleart.com (Shishas and sew-on shisha covers, also fabric supplies)

Suppliers UK

Delicate Stitches, 339 Kentish Town Road, London NW5, tel. 020 7267 9403.(*Stock entire range of DMC rayon hand embroidery threads, large stock of embroidery supplies of all types.*)

Liberty plc, Regent Street, London SW1, tel. 020 7734 1234 (*Large range of exclusive fabrics of all kinds, including printed silks and Liberty prints; good haberdashery department.*)

Borovick Fabrics Ltd, 10 Berwick Street, London W1, tel. 020 7437 2180 (*Good range of plain-coloured raw silks, Indian silk and lurex mix, exotic fabrics.*)

Wolfin Textile Ltd 64 Gt Titchfield Street, London W1W 7QH 020 7636 4949. (*This shop stocks 'basic' textiles: cotton calicoes, drill, cotton lawn, domett.*)

Norman Lyons & Co, 106 Cleveland Street, London W1, tel 020 7380 1515 (*Fascinating shop on the edge of the rag-trade district, large selection of fashion fabrics, mostly synthetics, often in industrial widths.*)

John Lewis plc, Oxford Street, London W1, tel. 020 7629 7711 (*Fabrics, quilting supplies, cushion pads.*)

Rainbow Textiles, 98 The Broadway, Southall, Middlesex, tel. 020 8574 1494 (*Silks and exotic fabrics.*)

De Haviland Embroidery, Monomark House, 27 Gloucester Street, London WC1 3XX, tel. 020 7289 2123 (*Beautiful random-dyed or plain hanks of rayon hand-embroidery thread. The yarn can be dyed to match. Mail order only.*)

Silken Strands, 20 Y Rhos, Bangor, LL57 2LT, Tel/fax 01248 362 361 (*Carry varied stock of hand and machine embroidery threads, also good-quality shishas. Mail order only.*)

Bead shop, 21a Tower Street, London WC2, tel. 020 7240 0931 (*Huge range of beads of all types, semi-precious stones, specimen beads from around the world.*)

Lavenders of London, Florists Sundries, Unit 12, Metro Centre, St Johns

Index

appliqué 8, 25, 52, 68, 84, 92

batting/wadding 25, 62, 72, 74, 88
beading 14, 15, 44, 45, 55, 70, 71, 78, 80
Bengal 8, 40
Bihar state 8, 40
blocking of work 115, 122, 123
bobbin case 19, 21
buttonhole stitch 18, 31, 32, 33, 43, 44

chain stitch 18, 31, 32, 33, 43, 44, 112
  bi-coloured 32, 33, 43, 44
channel, hanging see sleeve, hanging
chevron stitch see herringbone stitch
colour 63, 64, 75, 78, 80, 82, 102, 106, 107, 125
conservation 63, 122, 125, 126
cotton lawn 19, 22, 25, 48, 53, 68, 70, 82, 84, 107, 120
crazy stitch 49, 60, 90, 100
couched work 45, 78
cushion edging, piped 116, 120
  corded 116, 121

daisy stitch 19, 32, 33, 43, 44, 75, 97
darning stitch see running stitch
designers, Indian modern 12
domett, 25, 75, 82 86, 98, 102, 104, 107, 115

embroidery 8, 10, 71
  hand 14, 15, 20
  Indian 8, 10, 12, 14, 28, 29, 30, 32

fabric, man-made 24, 82, 106
  fabric, synthetic see man-made
fagotting stitch 20, 50, 55, 76, 78, 97, 112, 116
feather stitch 18, 32, 33, 55, 70, 107, 108

feed dogs 20, 50
filling or speckling stitches 33, 34, 107, 115
frame, embroidery 21, 22, 48, 62
framing of work 101, 122, 123
French knots 19, 33, 34, 44
fusible webbing 25, 52, 75, 84, 86

Gujarat 8, 10, 28

herringbone stitch 31, 33, 34, 68, 70

iconography, Hindu/Buddhist 63, 101

machine embroidery 14, 20
  free-motion 15, 20, 21, 48, 50, 78, 92, 102
motifs, embroidery 15, 43, 112

objects, found 45, 68

patchwork 14, 24
  patchwork, cathedral window 12, 56, 80
  crazy 8, 15, 24, 50, 55, 68, 75, 76, 80, 82
  embellished 14, 15
  seminole 96, 120
  strip 58, 84, 116
  Suffolk puffs 70
  tumbling blocks 12, 24, 60, 100, 102, 104
peepul leaf skeletons 42, 45, 101, 110, 112, 114
prairie points 98
presentation, work 63, 65, 122, 124

quilting 8. 38
  hand 14, 19, 62, 74, 78, 102, 104, 107
  kantha 8, 12, 18, 33, 36, 40, 42, 70, 78, 80, 108, 110, 112
  machine 19, 62, 74, 88, 90, 98

quilts, American 10, 12, 36, 38

rabari tanka 33, 34
Rajasthan 8, 28, 29, 30, 92
ribbon, embroidery 18, 19, 44, 75
ruching, double 80, 92
running stitch, hand 8, 33, 38, 44, 62, 112, 114
  machine 48
sashing 62, 65, 72, 76, 78, 80
satin stitch, machine 20, 21, 50, 53, 55, 75, 86, 88, 92, 115
sewing machine, 20, 96
  accessories 21, 48, 62, 121
  tension 19, 20, 21, 48, 62, 64, 65, 76, 115
shisha work 8, 18, 28, 29, 30, 31, 43, 44, 45, 70, 78, 80, 120
  method, practical 31, 43, 44, 45
silk 8, 19, 21, 22, 23, 24, 65, 70, 80, 106, 120, 125
sleeve, hanging 72, 77, 80, 92, 104, 124
spider stitch 33, 34, 97, 107, 108

stem stitch 32, 33, 43, 44
stitches, automatic machine 20, 50, 104

tassel-making 117, 117
tea, dyeing 24, 80, 82
textiles, Indian 10, 12, 32
  Mexican 10, 12, 29
texture 14, 24, 63, 64, 70, 82, 92, 125
thread 18, 19
  cotton 19
  metallic 18, 24, 48, 49, 50, 86
  monofilament 19, 45,
  polyester 19
  quilting 19, 62
  rayon 18, 75, 88
  sewing 19, 48,
  stranded cotton 18

zigzag stitch 20, 48, 49